A Primer
of Brief
Psychotherapy

A Primer
of Brief
Psychotherapy

John F. Cooper

W.W. NORTON & COMPANY · NEW YORK · LONDON

Printed in the United States of America

First Edition

Composition by Bytheway Typesetting Services, Inc.
Manufacturing by Haddon Craftsmen, Inc.
Book design by P.J. Nolan

Library of Congress Cataloging-in-Publication Data

Cooper, John F. (John Frederick), 1954–
    A primer of brief psychotherapy / John F. Cooper.
      p.   cm.
    "A Norton professional book."
    Includes bibliographical references.
    ISBN 0-393-70189-1
    1. Brief psychotherapy. I. Title.
RC480.55.C67   1995
616.89'14—dc20   94-45948   CIP

W. W. Norton & Company, Inc., 500 Fifth Avenue, New York, NY 10110
W.W. Norton & Company, Ltd., 10 Coptic Street, London WC1A 1PU

1 2 3 4 5 6 7 8 9 0

To Ann, naturally

Contents

Acknowledgments

Thank you to the following people who by virtue of thoughtful comments, kind indulgence and encouragement, or valued friendship have contributed to this book: Lynn Johnson, Ph.D., Wil Hass, Ph.D., Nancy Bologna, Ph.D., Robin Cooper-Fleming, Psy.D., Max Hines, Ph.D., John Brose, Ph.D., Joyce Chung, M.D., Bob Lopno, M.A., Joan Dickinson, Ed.D., and Bill O'Hanlon, M.S. Special thanks to Susan Barrows Munro of W. W. Norton.

Some humorous quotes, lacking proper attribution to their original sources, have been excerpted from *Anguished English* by Richard Lederer, published in 1987 by Dell; *The 776 Stupidest Things Ever Said* by Ross and Kathryn Petras, published in 1993 by Doubleday; and *The Viking Book of Aphorisms* by W.H. Auden and Louis Kronenberger, published in 1966 by Dorset Press. "Short Session" is reproduced with the kind permission of Neal Crosbie and Paper Sharks.

A PRIMER
OF BRIEF
PSYCHOTHERAPY

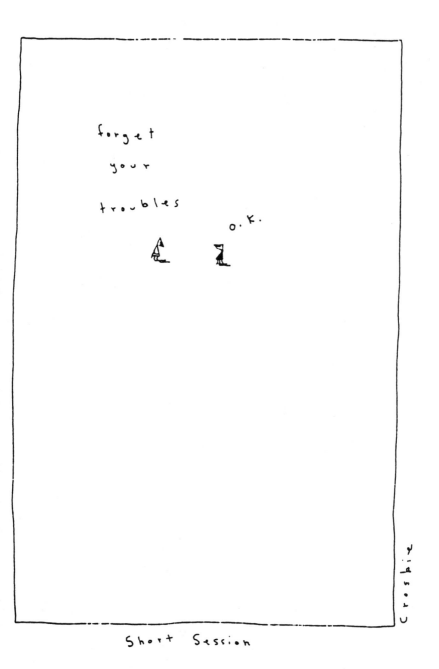

Of course it was not I who cured. It was the power from the outer world, and the visions and ceremonies had only made me like a hole through which the power could come.

— *Black Elk*

Festina lente (Hasten slowly).

— *Suetonius*

This book has too much plot and not enough story.

— *Sam Goldwyn*

1

Using the Primer

This primer is meant to be an enjoyable and useful guide to various aspects of brief psychotherapy (BT) and the practical application of a generic task-oriented BT model.

One idea of the primer is to distill and to summarize a large body of information into its essence. This has the potential advantage of maintaining reader interest while avoiding the sentiment unwittingly expressed by Lord Aberdeen to a guest: "My only regret is that your stay is not shorter."

On the other hand, this approach has meant forgoing some of the depth found in more complete studies of brief therapy. The primer should not be considered a substitute for a comprehensive review of the BT literature. (Many good resources, however, can be found in the bibliography.) Similarly, the primer is not intended as replacement for the knowledge and skill that come with varied experience and the best training and supervision you can obtain.

Another idea of this primer is to help organize and facilitate your own thinking about BT rather than to anticipate every treatment contingency or to follow a specific theory dogmatically. You are thus encouraged to work toward an effective personal model of efficient psychotherapy.

The heart of the primer is a practical outline of specific steps and strategies to use with clients in a prototypical session. In some cases, these steps are illustrated with examples. Readers may recognize the influences of solution-focused, systemic/strategic, cognitive-behavioral, interpersonal, and, to a lesser extent, dynamic therapy. However, the outline and examples are best viewed as a generic approach to BT built on the general principles underlying its various forms. More detailed illustrations of BT applications to various problems are found in a number of the sources listed in the bibliography.

To allow for rapid review, some sections begin with a summary of salient points with more detailed discussion following. Similarly, an informational quiz is offered at the outset as a way of presenting data supporting BT practice.

When you integrate any of the concepts presented here into your practice, do so in a manner that is comfortable for you. Try working on no more than one or two ideas at a time to see how you and your clients like them. You should feel free to make adjustments and improvise as necessary to get the results you want.

Ultimately, the goal and success of this primer lie in this: the thoughtful integration and selective application of the theories and techniques that work best for you and your clients.

BRIEF THERAPY INFORMATIONAL QUIZ

The quiz below is designed to present some information about BT in a way which stimulates your thinking. Answers to the quiz and a more detailed overview of brief therapy follow. Looking at them beforehand, however, is considered unsporting, even for outcome-minded brief therapists.

1. Brief therapy (BT) is a new concept. T/F

2. The number of specific BT approaches is approximately:
   (a) 1–5
   (b) 5–10
   (c) 15–25
   (d) 50+

3. BT is most aptly described as:
   (a) a plot by large third-party payers to deny necessary treatment to patients
   (b) the exclusive domain of HMOs
   (c) a viable treatment approach practiced willingly by a sizable number of competent clinicians
   (d) incompatible with other therapeutic approaches

4. The modal number of visits in outpatient public practice and possibly most other settings is:
   (a) 3
   (b) 8
   (c) 1
   (d) 10

5. The percent of patients who are likely to come only once to therapy is:
   (a) 30–55%
   (b) 5–10%

(c) 15–20%
(d) 20–35%

6. BT is less effective than long-term therapy. T/F

7. There is good research on long-term therapy outcomes. T/F

8. BT is concerned chiefly with limiting the number of therapy sessions used. T/F

9. Which of the following is a useful attitude for a brief therapist?
   (a) therapy ought to be the most important thing in a patient's life
   (b) therapists generally know what's best for a patient
   (c) reminding a patient frequently of time limits or hurrying toward a goal facilitates better outcomes
   (d) patient resistance or denial should either be ignored as nonexistent or doggedly confronted as masking the real issue
   (e) none of the above

10. Which of the following has the fewest elements of an intrinsically BT?
   (a) interpersonal therapy
   (b) cognitive-behavioral therapy
   (c) traditional psychoanalysis
   (d) strategic family therapy

11. The average number of patient visits in a course of psychotherapy is approximately:
   (a) 22–26
   (b) 6–8
   (c) 10–12
   (d) 16–18

12. Which of the following is NOT a standard BT technique?
    (a) reframing
    (b) careful history-taking
    (c) ignoring the initial complaint in favor of the real problem
    (d) joining
    (e) cognitive restructuring

13. Therapists are generally in agreement with patients about how many sessions they need. T/F

14. Treatment drop-outs are almost exclusively the result of treatment dissatisfaction. T/F

15. Which of the following is NOT an essential feature of BT?
    (a) rapidly establishing rapport
    (b) defining a treatment focus and plan in the first session
    (c) a concern with pattern interruption
    (d) reliance on existing patient and community resources
    (e) emphasis on change within the "here and now," implemented in small, clear, achievable steps with recognizable outcomes

16. BT is contraindicated with personality disorders. T/F

17. Brief therapy is contraindicated in the presence of concurrent substance abuse or dependence. T/F

18. Which is (arguably) the LEAST important question in BT?
    (a) Why now?
    (b) Why?
    (c) So what?

   (d) Now what?
   (e) What?

19. BT is contraindicated in the treatment of more severe disorders such as schizophrenia or bipolar depression. T/F

20. BT emphasizes therapeutic technique more than relationship development. T/F

QUIZ ANSWERS

1. **False.** Freud actually saw many patients for a few visits (Bloom, 1992). Ferenczi (1920) pushed for more rapid analytic approaches, while Alexander and French (1946) pioneered shorter term work with large populations. On a more philosophical note, the client-oriented approach was foreshadowed by Socrates, who practiced cognitive "midwifery," in which questioning was used to elicit wisdom which already existed in his students.

2. **D.** (Bloom, 1992; Budman, Hoyt, & Friedman, 1992; Koss & Butcher, 1986). *The idea of "brief therapy" really refers to the common treatment principles and underlying values of a large and growing number of specific approaches.* Most brief therapies can be roughly grouped according to characteristics associated with cognitive-behavioral (including strategic-structural) or psychodynamic thinking.

3. **C.** But A is more fun to talk about. There could be a conspiracy by insurers to deny necessary treatment but this has been difficult to prove unequivocally. More obviously, certain coverages or diagnoses are excluded to make policies more affordable for purchasers and

more profitable for payers. The questionable wisdom of this appears to have escaped the marketplace.

4. **C.** (see Bloom, 1992; National Institute of Mental Health [NIMH], 1981).
5. Trick question. Answers **A** (see Hoyt, Rosenbaum, & Talmon, 1992; Talmon, 1990) or **D** (see Pekarik, 1990a; Pekarik & Wierzbicki, 1986) are acceptable. Essentially, then, between 20–55% of patients are likely to come once to therapy.
6. **False.** But this could be a trick question. See definitions of long-term and short-term treatment discussed below and in Budman and Gurman (1988). Koss and Butcher (1986) found few studies directly comparing short-term and long-term therapy, and these had equivalent outcomes. A recent trend, however, appears to favor treatment with cognitive and behavioral components for many disorders (see Lambert & Bergin, 1994; Shapiro & Shapiro, 1982). The comparability of outcomes is also a matter in dispute for a variety of methodological and practical reasons. Most important and troublesome is the continued use and comparison of atheoretical or normative data to unique and specific situations (Beutler, 1991; LeShan, 1990; Persons, 1991). The most commonly referenced study in favor of long-term treatment is Howard, Kopta, Krause, and Orlinsky (1986) who found a steady increase in therapy benefits over time. However, this study is criticized by Pekarik (1990b) for its reliance on nonstandard practice. Specifically, the studies included had median visits far exceeding the norm in private practice or public mental health, emphasized therapist-rated outcomes, used "unusual" settings and were limited to dynamic and "interpersonal" approaches. Even Howard et al. (1986; see also Orlinsky

& Howard, 1986) found that treatment gain was disproportionately associated with earlier sessions when client
ratings of improvement were considered.

7. **False.** (Koss & Butcher, 1986; Pekarik, 1990a,
1990b). In fact, most therapy research concerns "un-
acknowledged" brief treatment with patients of less
than 20 visits. Moreover, the notion of what consti-
tutes long-term therapy is unclear.

8. **False.** BT is primarily concerned with providing good
treatment outcomes in the most efficient way possible.
BT has less to do with the number of sessions used, in
some cases this being more than "long-term" approaches in a given period (Budman & Gurman,
1988), than with how efficiently they reach a desirable
outcome. Some clinicians (e.g., Butler, Strupp, &
Binder, 1992; Mann, 1973) advocate setting or negotiating time limits beforehand to facilitate focus, while
others do this more implicitly by suggesting early and
regular evaluations of progress (Johnson, 1991a,
1991b). Some research supports the idea that explicitly defining time limits is therapeutic (e.g., Sledge,
Moras, Hartley, & Levine, 1990). However, *therapy
that feels pressured or rushed is not well-done brief
treatment.*

9. **E.**

10. **C.** The passive, vaguely authoritarian approach in
some analytic work, primary emphasis on understanding or resolving internal conflicts not in a patient's
awareness, often vague goals and outcome criteria,
assumption of resistance and the assumed need for
lengthy, frequent, and otherwise rigidly or arbit-
rarily scheduled treatment are inconsistent with most
BT.

11. **B.** (Garfield, 1986, 1994).

12. **C.**

13. **False.** Pekarik and Finney-Owen (1987) found therapists believed patients needed three times the number of sessions that patients themselves estimated. Patient estimates are far closer to the actual number of average visits in outpatient treatment (see Budman & Gurman, 1988; Pekarik, 1990a).

14. **False.** This is a complex phenomenon with multiple, probably interactive variables (Garfield, 1986, 1994) ranging from the interpersonal to the convenient. Many drop-outs appear satisfied with their progress but fail to communicate this (Bloom, 1992; Pekarik, 1990a). A conscientious brief therapist might still follow up with drop-outs. Intervening actively, concretely, and positively in the intake can have a salutory effect on patient satisfaction and retention (Adams, Piercy, & Jurich, 1991; Mohl, Martinez, Ticknor, Huang, & Cordell, 1991; Sledge et al., 1990).

15. Trick question. **All are characteristic of BT.**

16. **False.** Some brief therapists (e.g., Pekarik, 1990a) dismiss treating personality as irrelevant to treating specific patient complaints, especially since the evidence supporting personality change is scant. Winston et al. (1994), however, report success with various personality disorders in a controlled study using two arguably "brief" (40-session) dynamic approaches. Leibovich (1981) and Lazarus (1982) report success treating severe personality disorders dynamically, probably because help is offered in concrete, limited, "respectful" ways (Donovan, 1987). Donovan (1987) notes that although brief dynamic therapists have historically excluded difficult personalities from treatment, working with "pathogenic beliefs" allows for treating most patients briefly. Beck et al. (1990) observe that in working with personality disorders, cognitive-behavioral therapy is focused not directly on

personality but on other specific problems related to personality, such as self-efficacy. This in turn shows promise in facilitating broader personality changes. Budman and Gurman (1988) outline an integrated way of dealing briefly with personality disorders that "intrude" in therapy, while Shearin and Linehan (1989) articulate a "metaparadoxical" approach with borderline personality disorder that is compatible with BT principles.

17. **Judgment call.** Budman and Gurman (1988) follow a fairly standard practice in not doing mental health treatment with many substance abusers. There are well-reasoned arguments against doing this from both pharmacologic and therapeutic standpoints (e.g., Dubovsky, 1993; Gitlin, 1990). These highlight, for example, the difficulty of separating depression from the effects of excessive alcohol intake. However, excellent discussions of working productively with substance abusers in cognitive (Beck, Wright, & Newman, 1992) and solution-focused (Berg & Miller, 1992b; Todd & Selekman, 1991) ways have been published. These emphasize accurate assessment of motivational levels for any behavior changes (see Prochaska, 1992), cooperatively engaging patients at the level they are willing to change, and capitalizing on these successes to move toward recovery.

18. **B.** Contrary to strict strategic thinking, asking "why" can be important for ruling out organic contributions to behavior, such as hypothyroidism to depression, or understanding a client's thinking in order to design an appropriate intervention. It also has facility, used by the therapist, as a way of "leading" strategically to a new client awareness. Beyond this, spending too much time on the "why" of behavior, especially with obsessive clients, often becomes a substitute for actually

doing something about a problem (Watzlawick, Weakland, & Fisch, 1974). When tempted to ask "why" too often, the best solution may be for the therapist to lie down until the urge to form a hypothesis goes away (O'Hanlon & Wilk, 1987). The other questions, in general, are better designed to move therapy forward.

19. **False.** There are no substantial empirical or demographic contraindications for BT (Bloom, 1992). Some brief therapists, especially dynamic therapists, may screen heavily for appropriateness, but this is theoretically-based and conveys a limited understanding of BT and working with chronic or "difficult" patients. The same limitations to effectiveness, such as organicity, coherence, or motivation, apply to long-term treatment as to BT (Bloom, 1992; Budman & Gurman, 1988). Moreover, the number of problems inherent in difficult patients indicates the use over time of such BT hallmarks as establishing treatment priorities; focusing; taking small, concrete steps; regular evaluations of progress; and the use of adjunctive support. Specific illustrations of working with difficult patients can be found in BT literature (e.g., Freeman & Dattilio, 1992; Wells & Gianetti, 1990, 1993).

20. **False.** *Technique, while important, is subordinated to the development of a positive working relationship.* If there is misunderstanding about this point, it may have roots in overzealous BT workshop presenters or writers who have failed to call sufficient attention to the importance of relationship development. Therapists are in charge of, but not solely responsible for, how the relationship is formed and treatment is negotiated.

2

What Is Brief
Therapy?

"Brief therapy" simply means therapy that takes as few sessions as possible, not even one more than is necessary, for you
to develop a satisfactory solution.

— Steve de Shazer (1991a, p. x)

SUMMARY OF KEY FEATURES

*Brief therapy takes many forms but is characterized by
the planned use of specific concepts and principles in a
focused, purposeful way* (Wells, 1993). It emphasizes efficiency as well as efficacy. Underlying its variety, BT shares
a set of clinical features and a value orientation (Pekarik
1990b).

BT's *technical features* include:

1. Maintenance of a clear, specific treatment focus;
2. A conscious and conscientious use of time;
3. Limited goals with clearly defined outcomes;
4. An emphasis on intervening in the present;
5. Rapid assessment and integration of assessment within treatment;
6. Frequent review of progress and discarding of ineffective interventions;
7. A high level of therapist-client activity;
8. Pragmatic and flexible use of techniques.

The *shared values* of BT include:

1. An emphasis on pragmatism, parsimony, and least intrusive treatment versus "cure";
2. A recognition that human change is inevitable;
3. An emphasis on client strengths and resources and the legitimacy of presenting complaints;
4. Recognition that most change occurs outside of therapy;
5. A commitment that a client's outside life is more important than therapy;
6. A stance that therapy is not always helpful;
7. A belief that therapy is not "timeless."

Usually, "brief" therapy is defined in contrast to "long-term" therapy. Both concepts are routinely ill-defined solely in terms of elapsed calendar time or total number of visits. In practice, long-term treatment is often intermittent, while technically brief treatments may occur episodically over years with challenging problems such as severe abuse or trauma (see, for example, Dolan, 1991).

The picture becomes confusing considering that long-term and brief treatments share many common processes, including specific therapist activities such as the use of interpretation and nonspecific factors such as support and reassurance (Koss & Butcher, 1986). Further, a consensus is emerging that the interaction of interpersonal and technical factors is inextricably linked to any effective treatment. The absence of good technique in BT, such as lack of focus or failure to examine the therapeutic relationship (Sachs, 1983), may be as unhelpful as failure to achieve Winnicott's satisfactory "holding environment" (Rubin & Niemeier, 1992).

While attempts have been made to define long-term therapy succinctly as recapitulating one's personal history with a stable figure (Budman & Gurman, 1988; Budman, Hoyt, & Friedman, 1992), brief therapy lends itself less readily to simple definitions. Part of the problem in doing so lies in the sheer variety of BT. Well over 50 forms exist (see Koss & Butcher, 1986, for a partial review) with the number continuing to grow. Nevertheless, *most brief therapies share some essential characteristics and a common value system as well as several common principles* (Bloom, 1992; Koss & Butcher, 1986; Koss & Shiang, 1994; Pekarik, 1990b; Wells, 1993):

1. *The maintenance of a clear, specific focus.* This is arguably the primary hallmark of BT. Multiple problems are given priorities. Changes in focus are negotiated. The therapist helps patients stay focused from session to session on what they are trying to accomplish in treatment. Confusion about purpose or progress is immediately addressed.
2. *Conscious and conscientious use of time.* Some therapists or insurers limit visits at the outset for motivational or cost reasons. Additionally, many disorders, such as unipolar depression (see Shaw, Katz, & Siotis, 1993) or panic disorder (e.g., Barlow & Craske, 1989) have been shown to respond specifically to structured,

time-limited interventions. Essentially, however, this principle means using time flexibly to meet the demands of a situation, rather than assuming that all clients need or want weekly 50-minute visits.

3. *Limited goals with clearly defined outcomes.* These are negotiated with the client and defined specifically within problem areas. Achievable, observable, behaviorally defined outcomes are important in order to increase optimism about and recognition of success. (See Csikszentmihalyi, 1990, for a discussion of how purposeful goal-setting contributes to a sense of well-being.)

4. *A focus on present stresses and symptoms.* Brief therapists do not ignore the effects of history or biology on problem development. Neither do they avoid spending some time with clients who want to gain an understanding of their past (the "why" of behavior). However, BT emphasizes making relatively rapid connections from the past to the present, because this is where change occurs (so we know "why"; now what?). It also recognizes that many people tend to be satisfied with "symptom relief" and leave treatment when they get it (e.g., Pekarik, 1983).

5. *Rapid initial assessment and integration of assessment to treatment.* Getting started right away has been characterized by some (e.g., Johnson, 1991a; O'Hanlon & Weiner-Davis, 1989, based on the work of Peters & Waterman, 1982) as "ready, fire, aim." As soon as there is sufficient information to justify a working diagnosis or hypothesis about problems, trial solutions are negotiated and attempted, thus initiating a continuous process of diagnosis through action (Wells, 1993). This tactic, like brief therapy generally, tends to benefit from therapist experience, confidence, and skill. It requires therapist willingness to be "wrong" at any given time and to make appropriate adjustments.

6. *The frequent review of progress and discarding of inef-*

fective interventions. A willingness to try "something different," even if it does not produce anticipated results, should not generally be framed as a failure. Rather, if you are being run out of town, get in front and make it look like a parade. After all, a failed intervention is another opportunity to define better solutions.

7. *A high level of client-therapist activity.* In a context of collaboration, therapists are active, even directive and challenging. Questioning, educating, and hypothesis-testing are common interactional components in BT. Clients are typically assigned "homework" (something specific to do or think about) to facilitate progress between sessions.

8. *The creation of a safe and comfortable environment for emotional expression.* Some brief therapists are deliberately evocative of affect as a "curative" factor, while other clinicians may place relatively greater emphasis on cognitive or behavioral contributions to change. Almost all brief therapists, however, try to establish an atmosphere of understanding and compassion which allows for appropriate emotional expression by clients.

9. *A practical and eclectic use of treatment techniques.* Matt Kramer (1989) suggests that technology in this country would be better used to serve, rather than to define, wine-making. As in wine-making, so, too, in brief psychotherapy. Familiarity with a broad range of current research and practice allows therapists to tailor treatment more efficiently, confidently, and competently to the individual needs of patients.

DIFFERENCES IN BT APPROACHES

Paradoxically, efforts at detailed enumeration or analysis of differences between various specific brief therapies often seem eventually to lead to their similarities.

While theoretical differences in approaches certainly exist, the extent to which these differences are "purely" applied in practice is unclear. In part, this may be because the originators (as well as imitators) of psychotherapy approaches are inimitable individuals—often strikingly so. Salvador Minuchin, for one, has quoted another, the iconoclastic Carl Whitaker, as saying that "what this country needs is a good dose of nontheory" (Neill & Kniskern, 1982, p. viii).

In practice, experienced clinicians tend to use interventions which are similar in utility and intent, if not form, but which also reflect their unique personalities, experience, and situational demands. Donovan (1987) provides an example of this. Trained as a brief dynamic therapist, he expands the applicability of this approach by challenging clients' "pathogenic beliefs," which he calls closer to a personality structure than a cognitive function. The similarity to a cognitive view, however, is striking.

Over-rigorous efforts to distinguish approaches from one another also risk unfairly dichotomizing them. Not uncommonly, for example, the highly interpersonal, albeit mostly implicit, nature of "strategic" therapy is ignored in favor of its technical aspects. Similarly, most dynamic approaches now consider interpersonal factors in therapy to be as important as intrapsychic ones (Bloom, 1992).

This being said, brief therapies may be broadly distinguished by their psychodynamic, cognitive, or strategic-structural features (Peake, Borduin, & Archer, 1988). Much of the variance between BT forms can arguably be accounted for by either psychodynamic or cognitive-behavioral theory, with interpersonal psychotherapy (IPT) (Klerman, Weissman, Rounsaville, & Chevron, 1984; see also Weissman & Markowitz, 1994) serving as middle ground (Bloom, 1992; see also Jones & Pulos, 1993). IPT places explicit emphasis on the role of interpersonal processes in change and attempts to link interpersonal problems to current client symptoms. Table 2.1 compares selected brief therapy approaches.

Brief Psychodynamic Approaches

As BT evolves, strategic-structural and cognitive-behavioral approaches appear to be gaining favor over dynamic approaches (Lambert & Bergin, 1994; Wells, 1993). Apart from issues of relative effectiveness, this may be because brief dynamic therapies place greater emphasis on the selection of motivated, functional patients, capable of insight, thus limiting their applicability. Dynamic BT is also characterized by emphasis on transference and countertransference; confrontation and interpretation of focal, intrapsychic conflict; and in most cases, the psychological importance of termination (Ursano, Sonnenberg, & Lazar, 1991).

The distinguishing features of a number of dynamic approaches are reviewed by Bloom (1992). Malan's (1963) emphasis on working with limited treatment goals, identifying focal conflict, and correct selection of appropriate patients has been a pervasive influence in dynamic BT. His notion of "brief," however, is 40 sessions. On the other hand, Mann's (1973) approach adheres strictly to a 12-session limit in order to facilitate the patient's confrontation of "reality."

Davanloo's (1979) transference interpretations tend to provoke anger but are designed to limit transference neurosis. He considers his approach broadly applicable, even to severe pathology, as does Sifneos (1992) of his "anxiety-provoking therapy," which is gentler and more supportive than its name suggests. The approaches of Wolberg (1980) and Gustafson (1986) (the latter sees treatment as a series of first sessions) are both non-doctrinaire.

Table 2.1

COMPARISON OF SELECTED BRIEF THERAPIES*

Approach	Client Acceptance Rate**	Basic Treatment Focus	Key Techniques
DYNAMIC			
Mann	low	separation anxiety	transference interpretation
Davanloo	low	pre-oedipal, oedipal conflicts	confrontation, interpretation
Gustafson	low to moderate	"faults" produced from early trauma	empathic companionship; interpretation
Wolberg	moderate to high	presenting complaint	flexible; interpretation
Sifneos	low	oedipal conflicts	confrontation; interpretation
INTERPER-SONAL	moderate to high	interpersonal role disputes, transitions, deficits; grief	communication and decision analysis; expansion of options
COGNITIVE-BEHAVIORAL			
Beck	high	cognitive distortions	collaborative empiricism; cognitive restructuring
Ellis	moderate to high	irrational beliefs	rational disputation; homework
STRATEGIC			
Erickson	high	presenting problem	direct, indirect suggestion
Solution-focused	high	intrinsic solutions to presenting problems	strategic questioning; use of exceptions

*Adapted in part from Donovan (1987).
**Estimated rates based on authors' clinical reports, other commentaries, or available selection criteria.

Wolberg, in particular, incorporates "teaching, relaxation tapes, hypnosis, homilies, direct suggestion, psychoactive drugs, catharsis, faith, counting on good luck, dream interpretation, and crisis intervention" (Bloom, 1992, p. 42)!

Cognitive-Behavioral and Strategic Approaches

In contrast to dynamic brief therapies, cognitive-behavioral theories emphasize assessment and relief of current problems, use a variety of empirically-based techniques to achieve mutually determined goals, and typically strive for self-efficacy (Peake et al., 1988). Increasingly, these approaches are moving toward a constructivist, rather than strictly empirical view of treatment; that is, treatment effectiveness is enhanced by working within the reality of personal meanings that people create (Mahoney, 1993).

The therapies in this group are perhaps more numerous and diverse than dynamic approaches; yet like many dynamic therapies they are often associated with particular practitioners, many of whom have trained or worked together.

Strategic therapy, for example, has substantial roots in the work of Gregory Bateson (e.g., Broderick & Schrader, 1981) and Milton Erickson (e.g., Cade & O'Hanlon, 1993; Fisch, 1990; Lankton, Lankton, & Matthews, 1991; Zeig, 1982). Erickson's deemphasis on pathology and directive (but often indirect and metaphorical) style based on hypnotic paradigms is further elaborated in Haley's (1991) pragmatic problem-solving approach. Haley, in turn, has strong connections to Minuchin (Aponte, 1992; Minuchin & Fishman, 1981), whose "structural" approach to family treatment emphasizes resolution of specific, immediate problems by altering the transactional process that reveals and maintains them.

The MRI approach (e.g., Fisch, Weakland, & Segal, 1982; Segal, 1991; Watzlawick, Weakland, & Fisch, 1974; Weakland & Fisch, 1992) (to which Haley, Bateson, and Erickson also have connections) differs from structural therapy in that, even though problems are viewed as interactional and systemic, the resolution of the presenting complaint is done by narrowing the treatment focus to specific behaviors. How a behavior is seen as a problem, by whom, and what has been tried to fix it become important, as does working within the client's reality, considering how the problem is maintained by efforts to solve it, and reframing the problem.

Single-session therapy's (Hoyt et al., 1992; Talmon, 1990) "metatheoretical" perspective emphasizing the first session and Yapko's (1992) emphasis on hypnotic paradigms, pattern interruption, and rebuilding are further variations of this approach.

An important variation of strategic therapy, solution-focused brief therapy (de Shazer, 1985, 1988, 1991b; O'Hanlon & Weiner-Davis, 1989; Berg & Miller, 1992b; Walter & Peller, 1992), has emphasized building on exceptions to the presenting problem and making transitions rapidly to the identification and development of solutions intrinsic to the client or problem.

Budman and Gurman (1988) emphasize an integrated developmental approach with interpersonal and existential elements focused on the treatment question, "Why now?" Reid (1990) has proposed an integrative model utilizing problem-solving, dynamic, behavioral, cognitive, and structural components.

The inherently brief therapies associated with Beck (1976) and Ellis (Ellis, 1992; Ellis & Grieger, 1977) emphasize changing cognitive processes to achieve a desired outcome. These have contributed to the formation of "cognitive-behavioral" approaches (see Freeman & Dattilio, 1992; Hawton, Salkovskis, Kirk, & Clark, 1989; Hollon & Beck, 1994; Lehman & Salovey, 1990) with their systematic, specific, often rigorous documentation, hypothesis-testing, and incorporation of behavioral and social-learning paradigms.

THE VALUE ORIENTATION OF BRIEF THERAPY

> The idea that we could focus on our internal healing strengths simply does not occur to most people. Even more rare is the insight that if the cancer doesn't disappear, that too often can be acceptable and right.
>
> — *Larry Dossey (1993, p. 34)*

The practice of psychotherapy is inextricably linked to the values and beliefs of its practitioners. It is therefore imperative that therapists be clear about their own values to avoid unnecessary or unhelpful conflicts within themselves or in their work.

The following list (adapted from Budman & Gurman, 1988) reflects some dominant values in long-term and brief treatments. *Before proceeding, check the numbers below that correspond most closely to your own thinking.*

1. Therapy needs to change basic character in order to be effective.
2. Therapy is pragmatic, parsimonious, and strives to be unintrusive; small steps often lead to bigger changes.
3. Significant psychological change is unlikely in everyday life without therapy.
4. Psychological change and development are inevitable. Almost all behavior has utility and a potentially positive dimension. "Cure" is usually an irrelevant concept.

5. Presenting problems almost always reflect more basic pathology that can, and should, be changed therapeutically.
6. Client strengths and resources should be emphasized in therapy; presenting issues are to be taken seriously, though not always at face value.
7. Therapists should "be there" for client change.
8. Much, if not most, client change happens outside of therapy.
9. Therapy has a "timeless" quality which requires willingness to wait for change.
10. The timelessness of therapy is not generally acceptable.
11. Psychotherapy is almost always useful or benign.
12. Psychotherapy is sometimes helpful, sometimes harmful.
13. Therapy ought to be the most important thing in a client's life.
14. A client's life outside of therapy is more important than therapy.

To the extent that you picked *even* numbers, your values and beliefs are likely to be compatible with a BT orientation. If you did not check many even numbers, it may be useful to examine the basis of your clinical preferences before committing yourself to BT practice.

3

———————————

Why Practice
Brief Therapy?

Although the importance of a compatible value orientation to an effective brief therapist cannot be overstated, an understanding of the empirical rationale for brief treatment is also essential. The following key reasons serve to justify the practice of brief therapy.

1. Most patients do not stay in treatment long and many come only once, suggesting the need for treatment to make a rapid difference to them.
2. BT corresponds to most patients' expectations of treatment.
3. Most outcome data suggest that *planned* BT is at least as effective as long-term treatment across a wide range

of clients and problems for which it is viewed as the treatment of choice.

4. BT appears to minimize many of the factors associated with early drop-out.
5. Increasingly, third-party payers and regulatory agencies are demanding both efficiency and effectiveness.
6. BT is ethically consistent with the health care principles of patient autonomy, informed consent, and beginning with the least intrusive treatment.

Briefer forms of psychotherapy have gained increasing recognition in recent years, fueled by a number of factors. Significant among these is a perceived rise in mental health care costs. Consequently, there has been increased concern, especially among large third-party payers, that treatment be efficient as well as effective (Broskowski, 1991; Cooper & Thelen, 1991; Townsend, 1992). This has resulted in "population-oriented practice management," commonly associated with managed mental health care, in which treatment is made available to, and utilized by, large numbers of people (Sabin, 1991).

In the last twenty years HMO mental health care has become a distinct form of practice. These programs typically share the following characteristics: (1) an emphasis on accessibility (not always achieved); (2) a preference for outpatient care; (3) interaction with medical settings; (4) groups versus solo practice; (5) eclectic treatment methods; and (6) an emphasis on brief forms of therapy for diverse populations (Bennett, 1988). Although BT appears to have been co-opted by HMO practice, it may enjoy more widespread acceptance as its viability beyond the boundaries of managed health care is better understood.

At present, the degree of successful adoption of planned

BT in general practice is unclear. There are varying indications of practitioner acceptance of BT combined with apparent needs for more training (Budman & Gurman, 1988; Koss & Shiang, 1994; Wells, 1993).

However, the viability of BT is succinctly and substantially justified by data which suggest that practitioners see their outpatients for a relatively small number of visits (6–8; Garfield, 1986, 1994) regardless of other factors. This relatively small number of visits corresponds closely to the estimates of patients themselves (not necessarily therapists' estimates) of how many visits they will need for treatment (6–10; Garfield, 1978; Pekarik & Finney-Owen, 1987) and to the fact that the greatest proportion of treatment gain is obtained early in a course of therapy (Howard et al., 1986; Smith, Glass, & Miller, 1980).

It is highly likely, moreover, that a therapist will only get one visit to make a difference to a patient, since this is the mode of outpatient practice. It is important to know how to make this opportunity count (Hoyt et al., 1992; NIMH, 1981; Pekarik, 1990a; Talmon, 1990). Further, a review of the "medical offset" literature suggests that even one therapeutic interview, let alone a planned course of BT, can substantially reduce the use of medical services by patients for a period of years (see Bloom, 1992).

Most outcome studies documenting positive therapy effects are of 20 visits or less (Budman & Gurman, 1988), implicitly supporting the viability of even unintentional brief treatment. Studies directly comparing long-term and short-term treatment effectiveness suggest equivalent outcomes (Koss & Butcher, 1986), making cost-efficiency a more decisive factor in treatment selection. Based on the major literature reviews of BT (see Bloom, 1992; Garfield & Bergin, 1988; Koss & Butcher, 1986; Koss & Shiang, 1994), a case can be made for the efficacy of BT across a substantial range of client populations and problems, often being the treatment of choice (Wells, 1993).

Contrary to the presumptions of many clinicians who associate BT with denial of care, brief treatment may actually be *more* consistent with ethical practice than much longer-term approaches. Specifically, it is consistent with the notions of using least invasive procedures first, informed patient consent (since treatment is collaborative), and respect for patient autonomy (presenting complaints are taken seriously and clients are considered the primary arbiters of treatment success) (Budman & Gurman, 1988; Pekarik, 1990a; Wells, 1993). BT may actually serve to reduce therapy drop-out rates (Pekarik, 1990a, 1990b; Sledge et al., 1990) possibly because of its consumer-orientation (see Epperson, Bushway, & Warman, 1983) and focused, if not explicit, use of time limits.

WHY NOT PRACTICE BRIEF THERAPY?

Despite "overwhelming" evidence (Bloom, 1990) of the effectiveness of briefer approaches (presumably properly done) with most kinds of people and problems, many clinicians hesitate to develop skills in time-sensitive treatments. This is especially true for those trained in long-term analytic or dynamic approaches (Davanloo, 1979) and therapists who work unhappily in managed care (Budman, 1989) or other settings where there may be pressure to declare oneself a brief therapist despite inadequate training or an incompatible value system.

Possible reasons for therapist reluctance to practice BT include the following:

1. Inattention to the actual nature of caseload activity in which relatively few demanding patients are noticed disproportionately (Pekarik & Finney-Owen, 1987).

Clinicians thus perceive that treatment takes longer for most people than it actually does.

2. The belief that more treatment produces more treatment gain (Howard et al., 1986) and that BT may thus be superficial in its treatment of serious psychopathology.

3. The therapist's belief that probing unconscious conflicts in an effort to make "permanent" or blanket changes is a better approach than treating problems overtly indicated by clients (Berkman, Bassos, & Post, 1988; Hoyt, 1987).

4. It may be "threatening" for clinicians to find that shorter treatments are as effective, if not more so, than long-term therapy in outcomes (Richardson & Austad, 1991).

5. Practitioners may feel their autonomy is threatened by increased external controls such as utilization review implemented by organizations concerned with documenting outcomes (Zimet, 1989) or minimizing expenditures.

6. Clinicians who do not take the time to inform themselves well about BT may make false assumptions about its nature. (At a presentation, an experienced family therapist commented to a BT trainer that he hadn't realized that BT was so systemic.)

7. The absence of graduate programs or systematic training protocols in BT (Crits-Cristoph & Barber, 1991; Pekarik, 1990b).

8. The demand for hard work; brief therapists need to be active, attentive, selectively focused, intuitive, and risk-taking (Hoyt, 1987), as well as broadly competent.

9. Therapist countertransference difficulties: ending with likeable clients; the need to be needed; or fearing loss of dependable income (Hoyt, 1987).

10. A perception that BT is impersonal, mechanistic, ma-
nipulative or formulaic in a way that other therapies
are not (Cade & O'Hanlon, 1993).

This last objection to BT is especially noteworthy for
two reasons: (1) It ignores the fact that in most effective
BT a premium is placed on establishing a positive relationship since efficient change seems less likely to happen without it; and (2) perceptions of warmth and caring probably
have less to do with technique or practice orientation than
with how these qualities are seen by clients (Rubin & Niemeier, 1992) or conveyed by individual therapists. Contrary to the expectation of some clinicians, for example,
clients have rated behaviorally-oriented therapists as more
open, genuine, and disclosing than their psychodynamic
counterparts (Staples, Sloan, Whipple, Cristol, & York-
son, 1976).

In any event, a reluctance to become familiar with brief
treatment means that opportunities may be lost for genuinely informed dialogue about the nature and provision of
quality care to patients. (It may be, as the Irish politician
Sir Boyle Roche said, that "only half the lies our oppo-
nents tell about us are untrue.")

Here's another example. Irvin Yalom (1989), a highly
regarded existential therapist with a long-term "depth" orientation, tells the story of his encounter with "Penny," a
woman disturbed about significant losses in her life. She
wishes to see him in the three months he has before he
takes a sabbatical. Against his better judgment, since he
believes three months of regular visits are inadequate for
"decent" therapy, Yalom sees her. Despite a good outcome
and a satisfied patient, Yalom remains dissatisfied regarding the depth of therapy he has achieved as insufficient to
manage "death anxiety." He sees the patient's rapid progress as exceptional, rather than examining further how he

helped her accomplish results in a comparatively short time. In other words, Yalom seems unable to reconcile the patient's experience with his own expectations and needs.

A compelling solution-focused brief therapy counterpoint to this approach with "death anxiety" is available on an audiotape in which a prostitute with AIDS wishes to "die well" (Berg & Miller, 1992a).

Experiment: Let patients (preferably not suicidal or psychotic) take the lead in scheduling their own appointments. *Prediction*: A significant number will choose, sooner rather than later, to be seen biweekly or at longer intervals. Those requesting more frequent visits will, upon noting progress, spontaneously decrease visit frequency. Even dependent patients will do this, if their nondependent behaviors are highlighted and built upon rapidly. They seem to say, as Dr. Samuel Johnson once told a companion: "Stay til I am well and then you shall tell me how to cure myself."

4

Brief Therapy Procedural Outline

This chapter is the heart of the primer, representing as much as possible a generic perspective. The outline is best viewed as a general approach to BT to which you should "graft" what we know from research and experience to be specifically helpful for particular clients and problems. Some short and specific technical illustrations are included.

The emphasis on a first session is deliberate. In effect, brief therapy may be seen as series of first sessions, bound gently but firmly (not rigidly) by a treatment focus.

PROCEDURAL OUTLINE SUMMARY

I. **Pre-intake tasks**
   A. Gather as much history as possible beforehand.
   B. If there is phone contact before the first session, help patients focus their thinking about treatment expectations.
   C. Be on time for the appointment and end promptly.

II. **First-session tasks**
   A. Form a positive working relationship.
   B. Find a treatment focus.
   C. Negotiate criteria for a successful outcome.
   D. Distinguish clients from non-clients.
   E. Identify client motivational levels and tailor interventions accordingly.
   F. Do something that makes a difference today.
   G. Negotiate homework.
   H. Leave time for questions/concerns. Assess the helpfulness of the session.
   I. Document the session.

III. **Subsequent session tasks**
   A. Review your mutual understanding of the presenting problem and the focus of the previous session.
   B. Review homework.
   C. Ask what is better since the last meeting and how it got that way.
   D. Do something specific to make a difference today.
   E. Negotiate new homework consistent with progress and goals.
   F. Assess the helpfulness of the session: Are people getting what they want?

IV. **Maintain gains**

V. **Ending treatment**

VI. **Documenting outcomes**

I. PRE-INTAKE TASKS

A. Gather as Much History as Possible Beforehand

1. *Have patients fill out a history form,* including questions about referral source, past treatment, medications, substance use, and reasons for coming in at this time. Consider a few questions or possibly symptom checklists which screen for suicidality or elicit focal symptoms. This saves time in the session.

2. "You can observe a lot by watching," as Yogi Berra said. *Pay attention to pre-session or waiting room behavior* (as well, of course, to in-session behavior). This will help facilitate your understanding of clients and may lead more rapidly to effective interventions.

Example: A married couple presenting with "communication problems" chats amiably in the waiting room but the wife seemed tense and tight-lipped during the intake, reminiscent of seething anger. A hypothesis was quickly, but tentatively, raised that the communication problem appeared related to discomfort with the consequences of expressed anger. It was further surmised, based on other behavior that seemed solicitous, that the wife was trying to be (unsuccessfully) "helpful" by protecting her husband from her anger.

B. If There is Phone Contact Before the First Session, Help Patients Focus Their Thinking About Treatment Expectations

For example, ask patients to think specifically about what would be different in their lives if treatment were successful for them. (Incidently, some brief therapists use the phone for a great deal of facilitative treatment. However, if you are feeling overwhelmed by the frequency of your contacts, make sure that you are not subtly communicating to clients that they cannot function without you.)

C. Be on Time for the Appointment and End Promptly

This is not just courtesy. It sets a work-oriented tone and an expectation that your time and relationship with the client are valuable and are to be treated as such.

II. First-Session Tasks

This section is the prototypical outline for operating briefly. As with BT generally, technique is important but must be subordinated to general treatment principles.

Keep in mind that while this task-orientation has direction and is somewhat sequential, it is not rigidly so. Tasks may overlap or serve multiple purposes. Thus, for example, a succinct, empathetic restatement of a client's problem conveys understanding (important to relationship building) while also serving to clarify a potential treatment focus.

Tip: Consider each session as whole in itself. Guide interventions by the nature of the presenting problem and three "metatheoretical" questions:

1. How is the patient stuck (what is maintaining the problem)?
2. What does the patient need to get unstuck?
3. How can the therapist facilitate or provide what is needed? (Hoyt et al., 1992, p. 62)

A. Form a Positive Working Relationship

It is critical for any therapist to learn how to do this rapidly and continuously. This is *not* to ignore the obvious value of relationship development over time, especially for more ambivalent clients or difficult problems. However, therapists often get a limited chance to make a positive impression, since people tend to make quick judgments about each other which are difficult to change.

It is also important to remember that forming a positive relationship with clients is an ongoing, interactive process, significantly contingent on the therapist's ability to engage clients helpfully in therapy from the start. Here are some suggestions:

1. *Consider spending a few minutes constructively getting acquainted.* This can serve as a kind of data collection, perhaps to complement history forms which often do not provide much useful therapy information in themselves.

2. *Do some therapy education.* Discuss mutual expectations of treatment, the process of therapy and such factors as time, cost, or treatment options.

3. *Ask how you can be helpful.* The typical response to this question is "I don't know." However, some people do know and they might like to be asked. More importantly, a tone is established that you are there as to be helpful as a consultant, not a miracle-worker. This question can be productively followed by a discussion of what would need to happen for treatment to be successful for clients.

4. *Use active listening, empathy, and language that demonstrates respect for each client's point of view.* Pace and use the client's language; that is, try to match, to a reasonable extent, a client's speech characteristics: rate, tone, latency, and inflection (Johnson, 1990). Especially use words, metaphors, images, grammar, and humor that reflect your understanding of the client's world (e.g., O'Hanlon & Weiner-Davis, 1989). These can then be used to motivate client action or demonstrate new ways to cli-

ents of seeing their "stories" (Friedman, 1992; Hudson & O'Hanlon, 1992).

Of course, this can be a challenge if you are helping someone like Sir Boyle Roche, who routinely said things like "I smell a rat, I see him floating in the air, but mark me, I shall nip him in the bud." Here's a better example of this principle: A mother described her son's demands of her as "like a little general's." She was then helped to describe and act like someone who was higher in rank than a little general.

5. *Find a one-sentence summary to repeat to clients, preferably in their language, which reflects your understanding of their most salient problem.* This may also suggest a treatment focus. *Example*: "So, is it fair to say that the more you spank Junior, the more defiant he gets and the more frustrated you become?"

6. *Find at least one thing to like or respect about each client or his or her coping and call attention to it.* Social psychology indicates that this may initiate a positive spiral of interaction (Aronson, 1992).

7. *Induce an expectation of improvement.* In this way, desirable placebo effects may be engaged, which may have either "additive" or salutory treatment effects in themselves (Goleman, 1993; Lambert, Shapiro, & Bergin, 1986). As corollaries to this strategy:

(a) *Stay positive.* This contributes to hope and, as Samuel Johnson observed, "hope itself is a species of happiness." Hope is also tied to the ongoing process of mutual respect and good therapeutic work (Beier & Young, 1984; Frank, 1974).

(b) *Maintain an air of confidence about achieving a reasonable outcome.* This may have a salutory effect on actual outcome (Beutler, Crago, & Arizmendi, 1986).

Unrealistic expectations, however, are not to be encouraged.

B. Find a Treatment Focus

This is, perhaps, the hallmark of BT. To paraphrase Yogi Berra again: If you don't know where you're going, you might not get there.

The focus of treatment in BT (what is it that we are going to do something about?) is collaboratively developed with the patient and is related to the concepts of assessment and diagnosis.

Formal diagnoses are typically associated with medical or "pathological" models of treatment and are therapist-derived. On the other hand, most patients do not come in saying, "I'm less concerned with my dysthymia right now than with my social phobia and avoidant personality disorder." It is therefore important in BT to develop diagnostic skills (see section I below on documenting treatment) while working within a client's perception of a problem.

A general strategy in achieving focus is to look for the cognitive, behavioral, and affective coping patterns of clients. Insofar as they become overly rigid and unhelpful, these coping patterns may become potential treatment targets.

Elaborating the variables below, known as "SORC," may help dictate an appropriate intervention (Giles, 1992):

(a) *Situations*: identifiable behavior patterns related to challenging circumstances. *Examples*: losses, illness, work stress.

(b) *Organic causes*: *Examples*: mitral valve prolapse as a contributor to panic, or hypothyroidism to depression.

(c) *Responses*: problematic thoughts, emotions, and behavioral reactions to something, possibly intrapersonal or interpersonal.

(d) *Consequences*: look especially for factors that may
inadvertently strengthen symptomatic behavior and
complaints.

Here are some other tips for achieving focus:

1. *Ask what has brought clients to treatment NOW
rather than earlier or later*. A common focus is on a tem-
porary setback in coping which departs from clients' typically adequate or satisfactory development.

2. *Ask what has improved since the appointment was
made that patients would like to keep improving*. It has
been suggested that perhaps 15 percent of patients show
pretreatment improvement (Howard et al., 1986). Investi-
gate what patients did to improve things and prescribe
more of the same.

3. *Determine at the OUTSET what would be tangibly
different for clients at the END of successful treatment*.
Ask this in various ways, as necessary, to get specific answers with observable outcomes. It is worth developing
this technique because skillful, rapid transitions from
problem identification to solution formation facilitate
overall efficiency in treatment. (See the sections below in
this chapter for examples.)

4. *If possible, jointly devise a succinct rule about client
behavior that can serve as a focus for intervention. Example*: A "rule" governing a man's unhelpful criticism of his
spouse is formulated this way: "If I criticize her often
enough, she'll do things perfectly." Interventions can then
be devised to challenge this belief or behavior.

5. *Define problems in specific terms amenable to*

change. As Socrates said: "The beginning of wisdom is the definition of terms." *Example*: If clients say they're "depressed," find out exactly what this means to them and how it is a problem. Fatigue, lack of pleasure, and sadness are more manageable than "depression."

In general, avoid unquestioned acceptance of broad, vague terms (e.g., "anxious" or "low self-esteem") or popular terms such as "codependency," which may be subject to the Barnum effect (Logue, Sher, & Frensch, 1992). The more specific description of anxiety as "heart-racing while speaking in front of a group" makes the problem clearer and more manageable.

6. *Find out how the presenting complaint is a problem for clients. Get agreement about the nature of the problem.* (Not all stated concerns are problems. Neither are all problems amenable to treatment.) *Example*: A client who casually stated that he was suicidal was asked how that was a problem for him. He acknowledged that it wasn't really a problem for him since he didn't intend to kill himself. It was, however, a problem for the hospital staff. They didn't understand the comfort thoughts of suicide gave him in dealing with his problem—the potential loss of his girlfriend.

It is important to determine the meaning or significance of a problem to a client. Example: A woman is asked what it means to her that her husband is having an affair. She replies that it means that something must be wrong with her. This perception then can become a potential treatment focus. (See Burns, 1990, for examples of the "vertical arrow" technique, which facilitates this understanding of meaning.)

7. *If multiple problems are identified, rank them in the order of importance. Focus first on the most important to the client.*

Tip: Many clients have difficulty articulating treatment goals. This is most productively treated as confusion that needs to be approached creatively rather than as denial or "resistance." This latter view risks setting up an unnecessarily adversarial relationship.

C. Negotiate Criteria for a Successful Outcome

Once problems have been identified, elicit from clients what would constitute a satisfactory outcome and translate that into goals/solutions. Consider doing this through sensitively paced questioning, using your own reactions to the client as a guide.

Tip: It is here that you may incorporate what we know from research and experience to be most helpful for particular patients or problems — thus, the "negotiated" aspect of reasonable outcomes.

(a) *Put solutions in positive, specific, achievable terms, using client language to facilitate change*:

   (i) *Turn negatively stated goals into positively stated goals. Example*: If clients say they are depressed and a goal is to "not be depressed anymore," ask what will be different when they're not depressed anymore in a way that suggests a positive focus. Clients might say then they will be "happier," which meets the criterion of positive focus but lacks specificity.

  (ii) *Make goals specific*. If clients say they want to be happier (instead of being depressed) find out what would be different when they're happier. What would others notice about them? Determine specifically what this means, perhaps as if in a videotape description. *Example*: Via questioning and negotiating, a client indicates she will know she is doing better when she is exercising three times a week, having dinner at least once a week with friends, and finding something each day to enjoy about her work. Treatment then focuses on how to make these things happen successfully.

(b) *Make goals/solutions achievable*:

(i) *Put goals within client control.* Paradoxically, this may require externalizing aspects of some problems, such as depression, anxiety, or self-criticism, which have become internalized. For example, in the latter case, linking an internalized self-critical voice with that of a real-life critical mother-in-law allows the intrapersonal, intropunitive problem to be treated more tangibly as interpersonal: "What would you like to say to your mother-in-law when she criticizes you?"

If possible, identify coping that has worked before with a similar problem. Otherwise identify something the client has not yet tried and is able and willing to do that may make a difference.

Example: A woman trying to get more free time for herself ineffectively nags her husband about his household duties. Alternatively, she is willing to try the idea of using joint funds (to which her husband contributes more!) to hire some help.

(ii) *Make treatment goals realistic and, if possible, measurable.* In working toward goals, identify the smallest possible changes that would make a difference and discuss how that might happen.

Example: A client rates his anger control as a "3" on a 10-point scale. His initial goal of not being angry anymore at his employer is negotiated to a more realistic goal of showing anger more constructively and criteria for this are established. The client indicates that he would be at a "4" if he could notice and write down specific situations that made him angry at work during the week.

Tip: Be sensitive to the power of questioning to shape therapy. To the extent that answers to problems come from therapists, they should be "reasonable" or along lines of education and reassurance. Otherwise therapists risk undermining clients' confidence in their own judgment, control, and intrinsic motivation (see McAuley, Poag, Gleason, & Wraith, 1990).

D. Distinguish Clients from Non-Clients

This is a critical but often underappreciated idea: *Not everyone who appears in therapy is a candidate for change.*

The concept of customers, complainants, and visitors (e.g., de Shazer, 1988; see also Berg & Miller, 1992b) is useful in determining "real" client status, particularly as it emphasizes working optimally with different stages of client motivation for change (see section E below).

Clients or "customers" are characterized in this framework by the acknowledgment of a problem and a willingness to work on it. Customers for change see themselves as being part of a solution.

"Complainants" will acknowledge a problem exists but do not see themselves as part of a solution. They are often described as "difficult" clients because they are genuinely distressed but commonly blaming or helpless since the solutions to their problems lie outside of themselves.

Family members trying to change alcoholics and many depressed patients, possibly owing to cognitive distortions or lack of energy, fit into this category.

An initial lack of clear goals does not define a complainant. The therapist's job is to help clarify objectives for all patients and put them, if possible, in attainable form. However, getting people to change when they are not ready or do not want to do anything different (even though they may be distressed) poses problems reminiscent of the story about the Boy Scouts: They were so anxious to do a good deed that they helped an elderly lady across the street even though she didn't want to go.

"Visitors" do not acknowledge that there is a problem. They often come at someone else's request or under pressure. The treatment of choice here is for the therapist to respect the patients' belief that their lives are sufficiently in order. For fun, you might inquire about the secrets of their success. More seriously, you might determine if they would be willing to help anyone who is distressed who may have accompanied them to treatment.

E. Identify Client Motivational Levels and Tailor Interventions Accordingly

Start by asking these questions:

1. Who is (most) willing and able to change?

2. What are they willing to do to change or to accept matters?

3. Can strategies be devised for non-clients?

There are five stages of change in addictive behavior which are useful to consider regarding motivation for change generally (Prochaska, 1992):

(a) *precontemplation*: no serious intent to change in the foreseeable future is apparent;

(b) *contemplation*: patients think seriously about change, but debate the pros/cons of doing so;

(c) *preparation*: patients intend to take action in the next month and have unsuccessfully taken action in the past year;

(d) *action*: patients actively modify behavior, experiences, or environment;

(e) *maintenance*: patients work to consolidate gains.

The last three stages above correspond to having a genuine client, while stage 2 roughly corresponds to the complainant and stage 1 to the visitor. The implication: *A different kind of intervention is required for each stage of change. Failure to recognize this may result in inefficient and ineffective treatment.*

Preferred strategies for intervening with non-clients reflect their relative lack of participation in the change process and include, variously:

1. Simply note some positive aspect of their coping without helping them change anything (since they're not ready).

2. Have them observe or think about some aspect of the problem, especially exceptions to a problem.

3. Find a problem, perhaps not immediately apparent, that the non-client is willing and able to do something about.

F. Do Something that Makes a Difference Today

1. *Listen actively and empathically.*

2. *Discuss the process of obtaining desired solutions.* Define the role of therapy and your role as a helper.

3. *Conceptualize or REFRAME problems in ways that suggest solutions.* Reframing is a desirable change in perspective which often leads to corresponding changes in

attitude and behavior (e.g., Weeks & Treat, 1992). Because of its potential for turning problematic behavior
rapidly on its head, reframing is well worth developing as
a basic skill. It is here, also that therapists can draw on
whatever rich understanding they have about the meaning
behind human behavior.

Tip: In reframing, look especially for positive intentions
behind problematic behavior, the positive function of
symptoms, or their positive unintended consequences—
whatever can genuinely be considered an alternative view
of a problem (Johnson, 1990; Weeks & Treat, 1992).

Example: A couple's fighting, subjectively distressful
but not otherwise harmful, is reframed as a form of intimacy and trust-building. Or, to distressed parents: "Your
son may have the belief that only by acting up can he
be assured of your love." In these cases, the behavior is
reframed, accurately (this is important) and more desira-
bly, as a component or a test of intimacy and love.

(a) *Normalize behavior or complaints*. While diagnostic
    terms may be useful between professionals, labeling
    people as pathological in session may overwhelm them
    or distance them from their humanity (Aronson,
    1992). Move away from simplistic or pathological la-
    bels toward more normal and confidence-inspiring
    ones. *Example*: "Panic" thus becomes a normal fear
    reaction, often to perceived danger, that comes at spe-
    cific, inappropriate, or inconvenient times.

(b) *Determine to what extent the complaint is really a
    problem that the client is willing and able to do some-
    thing about*. The question "How is this [presenting
    complaint] a problem?" can often clarify how some-
    thing is troublesome in a way that makes it more ame-
    nable to change. Sometimes the problem is someone
    else's that a client has adopted.

Example: A young woman is upset that her sister leaves her two children with their mother. One of the central questions of BT, "But how is this a problem for YOU?" (variously, repeatedly, and gently posed) eventually clarifies that it is her mother's problem.

4. *Consider immediate, active interventions.* These include role-plays, problem-solving, education, normalization of behavior, relaxation training, directives, and appropriate confrontation or interpretation. Or make useful adjunctive referrals.

5. *Build on exceptions to a problem. Example*: A self-labeled "codependent" woman, with lengthy prior treatment experience, felt despondent because she still couldn't say "no" to men. During their first session, the therapist kept remarking on how puzzling it was, then, that she had just managed to quit a male-dominated job she felt was demeaning to her. By the next visit, she had happily decided she was stronger than she had thought.

6. *Build on pretreatment gains if they have been noted.* Define what made a problem better and prescribe more of it.

7. *Determine and utilize past positive coping with similar problems.* Has this problem occurred before? What helped the client get through it? Can this be done again?

8. *Clarify whether clients are sufficiently motivated to do what is necessary to change a problem.* Some problems distressing to an observer, such as many obsessive-compulsive behaviors, may actually be ego-syntonic to the client. In these cases, a session may be spent doing nothing more than defining how uncomfortable someone is willing to be to get better.

9. *Notice (label) and allow, if not encourage, the appropriate expression of affect.* This may be helpful in communicating empathy and understanding patient coping. Moreover, it is possibly therapeutic in itself.

10. *If necessary, inform clients of the limits of therapy to help them.* Effective psychotherapy requires a problem amenable to change, a client willing and able to work toward change, and a competent therapist. To proceed in the absence of these factors may invite more problems.

G. Negotiate Homework

Whatever we learn to do, we learn by actually doing it.

— *Aristotle* (Ethics)

Homework consists of assignments designed to keep treatment focused and to help people use time productively between sessions. A particular value of homework is that it is consistent with evidence that goal-directed activity is essential to feelings of well-being (see Csikszentmihalyi, 1990).

Homework, broadly considered, has these functions: (1) to develop skills, such as identifying and recording automatic thoughts; (2) to disturb the system in which clients function and in which they are presumably "stuck" (Johnson, 1992).

An assumption in the latter case is that people know what they need to know to change, but are not organizing it productively. The homework in these instances often has a whimsical quality to it, such as flipping a coin or asking a people-pleasing client to poll all his friends about what he should do regarding a problem. Clients may be asked to change roles in family disputes or to alter the frequency, intensity, duration, or place of a symptom that seems out of their control (e.g., Ascher, 1989; Madanes, 1981; O'Hanlon & Wilk, 1987).

Homework tips:

1. *Be sure homework is consistent with client goals, values, abilities, and interests.* To the extent that clients are willing or active participants in formulating homework, compliance and meaningfulness will be enhanced.

2. *Fit the assignment to the appropriate level of motivation and client status.* "Active" homework should only be assigned to *clients*, as defined earlier. For non-clients, homework is probably best confined to "passive" assignments, as outlined in section E on motivation. These kinds of assignments should keep people positively engaged in treatment (if that is appropriate) while thinking about any advantages to changing their behavior.

3. *Homework should be specific and doable.* Consider the smallest possible behavioral step that might make a difference between visits. This is preferable to overwhelming people with expectations that their behavior should be remarkably different after they do their homework. Cognitive rehearsal or looking for an opportunity to *practice* the desired behavior rather than actually *do* it may help fearful or perfectionistic clients overcome their inhibitions.

4. *Determine cues to facilitate task completion and, if possible, a time and place.* ("How are you going to remember to do X?")

5. *Anticipate obstacles to doing the homework.* ("What's going to get in the way of your doing X?") Determine what motivates the client and use this to help overcome the obstacles.

Ideas for homework can be as varied as your imagination, personality, and client cooperation allow. The popular and professional therapeutic literature is full of them, ranging from the symbolic or ritualistic and culturally specific to standard cognitive-behavioral techniques (see Levy & Shelton, 1990).

Here's an example from Albert Ellis (Black, 1981). Ellis took a woman from a workshop audience who, upon questioning, was irrationally afraid of being rejected from graduate school. He had her transform her self-described internal feeling of "panic" to "disappointment" through an imagery exercise. Then he asked her to describe verbally the process she used to do this successfully. He asked her what she liked to do that she did daily, and she replied "Drink coffee." He then asked what she hated doing that she postponed, to which she responded, "Write letters." His highly directive homework:

> Now every day for the next 30 days, I want you to go through this same process. Intensify your feelings of panic, then change it to just disappointment. It won't take more than a few minutes. And you can't have a cup of coffee until you have done your imagery. And if midnight rolls around on any day for the next 30 days and you haven't done your homework, you have to write a letter. (p. 4C)

H. Leave Time for Questions/Concerns. Assess the Helpfulness of the Session

This requires experience and discipline. Practice ending a session five to ten minutes before you "have to" in order to discuss progress, review the essence of the session, or fine-tune homework. Make adjustments to the homework or your way of proceeding in the session, if necessary.

I. Document the Session

The "ready, fire, aim" quality of BT and the tendency to assess continuously do not mean that therapists are exempt from knowing how to do a good formal "work-up" of clients in medical model language.

Formal assessment and diagnoses are the common language of the mental health profession, the medical field, and insurance payers. Describing a clear, specific treatment plan based on an accurate assessment and an informal diagnosis, at the least, is important to patient care and may serve to clarify your thinking. However, a formal diagnosis and plan are what get treatment authorized.

Charting is not simply a matter of writing or dictating skill, but an indication of the clarity of your thinking, the quality of your therapy and the appropriateness of an intervention. It is also a method of communicating this to other professionals including, alas, attorneys. Its importance is therefore not to be underestimated. There are two basic forms for charting in BT: (1) the intake, or initial consultation report (see Table 4.1) and (2) the ongoing session note (see Table 4.2). In some settings a "termination summary" is also important.

The intake typically includes client identification data, a statement of the presenting problem, history of the presenting issue, history of past treatment and its outcome, relevant medical and chemical use history, *relevant* family history, mental status exam, initial assessment and diagnosis, and a treatment plan.

Note that, for the example in Table 4.1, details are included primarily as they concern the immediate problem or enable others to see why the diagnoses or treatment plans were made. Thus, lengthy family histories or detailed descriptions of events are usually not necessary and may even obscure more important data or foci.

Table 4.1

SAMPLE INTAKE NOTE

IDENTIFICATION: Emma H. is a divorced Caucasian female, 35, employed as a secretary. She has a 13-year-old son, Brian, who lives with her and has minimal paternal contact. The patient was referred by Dr. Zoe Loft of this clinic.

PRESENTING PROBLEM: "I've been depressed all my life." Ms. H. also reports more acute depressive and anxiety symptoms starting 3 months ago, when her son left for a month to visit his father and she was left to "confront" her relationship with her "non-committal" boyfriend of 3 years, Bubba. Dr. Loft placed her on Zoloft 150 mg. and Klonopin 0.5 mg. at night to which she has been only partially responsive. Her general treatment goal is "to feel happier."

HPI: Ms. H. cannot remember an extended period of euthymia. She notes prior episodes of depression during her divorce 4 years ago and 2 years ago when her current boyfriend left her for a time. They have reunited but he remains uncommitted to marriage, which the patient wants. Her current symptoms include being "sad all the time," though she rates her mood about a "4" on a 10-point scale. She notes "I don't enjoy anything," and has "little appetite," with a weight loss of about 5 lbs. initially, now stabilized. She reports guilt about being an inadequate mother and partner, expectations of being punished for no reason, harsh self-criticism, difficulty making decisions, and fatigue secondary to "waking up a lot." She has occasional nightmares, but wakes a few times a week with palpitations, in "cold sweats," and feelings that she just wants "to quit everything and get away." She has started to avoid going out with her close friends because she does not expect to have a good time.

Ms. H. notes she has historic difficulty saying "no" to people, taking great pains not to hurt them and avoiding conflict. Examples include wearing clothes "that aren't me" to please Bubba, letting a man whom she likes at work kiss her even though she was uncomfortable with it, and "spoiling" her son because she couldn't spend enough time with him.

Ms. H. believes she would be happier if (1) she were married to someone who accepted her as she was and was more "sociable"; (2) if she were in her own home rather than an apartment; (3) she could make a decision about whether to move on in her relationship; (4) she did not worry so much about money; and (5) she spent more time and set better limits with her son.

Her previous helpful coping has consisted of exercising, dressing as she likes, and spending "quality" time with her son and friends. It was observed with her that she appears to have considerable resilience and a clear idea of what is important to her in spite of her confusion.

(continued)

Table 4.1 Continued

PREVIOUS TREATMENT: None.

MEDICAL HISTORY: Non-contributory.

CHEMICAL USE HISTORY: Drinks moderately in social context. Has stopped caffeine intake which was moderate.

FAMILY HISTORY: Positive for paternal and fraternal alcoholism. The patient's mother has apparently been treated with antidepressants. The patient's parents divorced when she was 9. She has an ambivalent relationship with her father but feels close to her mother though she doesn't "see her enough."

MENTAL STATUS EXAM: Pt. was alert, oriented, and cognitively intact at the interview. She was prompt and neatly groomed. She was easily engaged with fair eye contact. Psychomotor status normal though she appeared physically tense. Speech occasionally halting but otherwise normal. Mood: sad and somewhat apprehensive. Affect: constricted. Denies suicidal or homicidal thinking or intent. Intelligence, insight, and judgment appear roughly in the average range.

ASSESSMENT AND DIAGNOSIS:
Axis I: 300.4 Dysthymic Disorder, probably early onset
              296.31 Major Depression, Recurrent, Mild (Provisional)
              300.01 Panic Disorder without Agoraphobia (Provisional)
              Rule out 300.02 Generalized Anxiety Disorder
Axis II: 301.90 Personality Disorder NOS (Provisional), dependent
              and avoidant features.
Axis III: None
Axis IV: Single parent; limited finances; conflicts with boyfriend
Axis V: Current GAF: 55
              Highest GAF last year: 70

PLAN: Continue meds per Dr. Loft. Treatment goals: (1) improvement and stabilization of mood; (2) increased assertiveness skills; and (3) establishing a sense of personal control over her life. Patient ideas for feeling better are noted in HPI and will serve as functional goals. Pt. agreed to homework of spending Saturday afternoon with her son, dressing one day as she wished this week and/or walking for 30 minutes three times this week to see what a difference these things make to her mood.

Much information can be detailed on history forms furnished to clients before the first session. It is especially important to note details consistent with BT principles: the current concern, patterns of coping, objectives in seeking treatment, exceptions to the problem's occurrence, client strengths, and specification of how possible solutions are going to be implemented.

III. Subsequent Session Tasks

The brevity of this section should not suggest that follow-up sessions are less important than initial contacts. Rather, it reflects the idea that the principles of first session tasks are consistent throughout treatment, though their form and emphasis may change as treatment demands. The follow-up tasks:

A. Review Your Mutual Understanding of the Presenting Problem and the Focus of the Previous Session

Continue with an established focus unless changes from focus are negotiated.

B. Review Homework

Build on any progress and address any difficulties immediately.

C. Ask What Is Better Since the Last Meeting and How It Got That Way

Note that this is not phrased *if* anything is better. The idea here is to orient clients to what is improving in their lives and capitalize on those improvements, even though problems are still acknowledged to be present.

D. Do Something Specific to Make a Difference Today

Some of these possibilities are noted in first-session tasks. Optimally, every subsequent session should have as a therapist goal, no matter how small, at least one tangibly useful intervention or interaction.

E. Negotiate New Homework Consistent with Progress and Goals

Sometimes the new homework may simply be doing more of what worked from the previous session.

F. Assess the Helpfulness of the Session: Are People Getting What They Want?

If not, determine what would be more helpful.

In charting subsequent sessions, many clinicians simply write a narrative paragraph describing what has happened in the client's life or in a particular session. However, we recommend some variation of the SOAP format because of its structural clarity and compatibility with BT (see Table 4.2).

S: This section refers to the client's "subjective" presentation. Record verbatim, if possible, one or two client statements that capture succinctly the client's current functioning in relation to the initial presenting problem (unless it has changed). Doing this forces the clinician to condense a client's presentation into a potential treatment focus.

Examples: "I had a better week" suggests a session focus on what the client did that improved matters, or "I'm angry all the time" suggests foci on identifying the dynamics and pervasiveness of the anger and possibly looking for exceptions to this perception.

O: This contains the "objective" focal content of the

Table 4.2

SECOND SESSION NOTES

S. "I had a good weekend with my son." "I'm doing a lot better."
O. Pt. spent a satisfying weekend with son and gave examples of assert-ive behavior with son and boyfriend. She told her boyfriend she ex-pects to be treated better and notes he has become more attentive and less critical. She notes improved mood with a day off from work "to spend for myself." Pt. speculated whether short-term memory and con-centration problems are medication related but it appears she may do too many things at once, feeling a lack of accomplishment as a conse-quence. We devised a task list strategy to see how this affects her con-centration/memory. She has exercised twice since last session.
A. 300.4, 296.31, 301.9 (Provisional). Some symptom moderation noted with assertive behavior.
P. 1. Use task list. 2. Compliment boyfriend specifically at least once on his positive treatment of her. 3. Spend a set time again with her son Sat. 4. Continue exercise.

session. This section should reflect how the subjective statement has been addressed specifically and may include mental status data.

A: This is an updated impression ("assessment") of how the client is progressing with respect to each diagnosis/ issue. Make sure you justify any revisions in diagnosis.

P: The "plan" should flow from clients' current status in achieving their objectives. This is where the homework should be specified in doable, observable terms. If you are unable to note a specific plan, consider whether there has been adequate focus in your session, or whether you have a client yet.

IV. Maintain Gains

Maintaining therapeutic gain in BT is a continuous pro-cess, often implicit in the overt recognition of client strengths and progress. *Some tips*:

1. *Continue to observe with clients what they do that is helpful to them*. This repeated observation and commentary should be designed to cultivate a sense of mastery and confidence in the coping of patients.

2. *Anchor desired behaviors to predictable sensory and experiential cues, both internal and external to clients.* Identify "reminders," especially naturally occuring ones, which clients can associate with desired behavior.

Example: A client wanted to improve his anger management in car traffic, among other places. He used the lighted brake lights of cars in front of him as a cue to "stop" his frustration level before it "accelerated" by physically relaxing and calming his thoughts.

3. *Plan for, and rehearse, relapses*. Anticipate this with clients by asking: "What might get in the way of your progress?" Devise appropriate strategies "as if" the obstacle were already happening. Take care in doing this that the emphasis is on the client's ability to cope rather than suggesting that a problem is necessarily going to recur.

V. Ending Treatment

This section is not titled "terminating treatment" for two reasons. The first is that "terminating" sounds unnecessarily violent. The second is because BT does not adhere narrowly to the idea of a final cure for most problems. Thus, ending therapy at a given time is not necessarily viewed as the end of treatment. It has been observed, after all, that life is often "just one darn thing after another" or, as Hobbes more cynically put it, "nasty, brutish, and short."

For practical and therapeutic reasons, treatment is often intermittent and developmental, extending to some clients over the course of years. In general, the ending of treatment reflects the fact that clients have (or, perhaps, have not) reached their goals and may find therapy useful again at some point in their lives.

Some brief therapists see the formal ending of treatment as critical because of the presumed importance to the patient of the therapist. Other clinicians give this less emphasis. Like their colleagues in family practice medicine, they expect that patients may come in periodically over time when they get "stuck." The idea of terminating a patient from this perspective is irrelevant.

In any case, if therapeutic progress toward clearly defined and mutually understood goals has been regularly noted, the ending of a course of treatment is typically self-evident. This is likely to be so even if the number of therapy visits has not been predetermined.

If, however, clients drop from treatment for unknown reasons, it is good practice to follow up with them. This will allow you to document accurately the status of treatment or take other appropriate action as necessary.

VI. Documenting Outcomes

Documentation of the progress and outcomes of treatment is increasingly a hallmark of good psychotherapy. This may be done by informal means such as asking clients if they were satisfied with treatment. Or, with respect to symptom change, periodically scaling intensity or frequency of a problem from 1–10 throughout treatment will give you and the client a measurable frame of reference for progress.

However, it is advisable and increasingly necessary to ratify satisfaction or treatment change with easily administered "objective" instruments. You should be able to find one or two that are appropriate for the specific problem being treated and compatible with the way that you work. For example, as a general indication of patient satisfaction, the Client Satisfaction Questionnaire-8 (CSQ-8; Nguyen, Atkisson, & Stegner, 1983) has excellent statistical values for a short instrument and is moderately correlated with other outcome measures. For problems or approaches emphasizing specific symptom change, the Symptom Checklist-90-R (SCL-90-R; Derogatis, 1983) could be considered.

Although some clinicians are uncomfortable with having their work evaluated by others, including clients, this kind of review is essential to continuing to improve the quality of your work. It is worth approaching openly and routinely.

5

Overcoming Obstacles to Progress: Tips and Techniques

This chapter deals with the problems of clients who for various reasons, including court-ordered treatment, resemble "complainants" and "visitors" as described in the previous chapter. Nothing, of course, works for everyone. Freud once told a patient that "fate would find it easier than I do to relieve your illness . . . much will be gained if we succeed in transforming your hysterical misery into common unhappiness" (Auden & Kronenberger, 1962, p. 217). When therapy is not progressing, the following, in no particular order, may be helpful to consider or reconsider.

Tip: It is important in using the more strategic/technical interventions that they be done in an appropriate context, with kindness, caring, and if possible, good humor. Practice them first with colleagues if you're not comfortable with them.

1. *Review mutual expectations of treatment.* Be sure goals are clear, client-generated, and manageable enough for success to occur. Perceived client resistance may be a reaction to poorly understood, overwhelming, or therapist-imposed objectives. If reparable therapist errors or misunderstandings are discovered, a sincere apology and clarification from the therapist can often lead to a more productive working relationship (see Omer, 1994).

2. *Make sure that you have "joined" each client in some way, that clients feel "understood" and are comfortable working with you.* Consider the advantages of genuine compliments (not flattery) about some aspect of client functioning *regardless of the client's motivation for change.* This may facilitate efficient intervention and continuance by: (a) circumventing fruitless power struggles; and (b) creating a positive connection.

Often, complainants and visitors, especially, have elicited negative reactions from others about their problems and may expect, or in fact experience, the same from therapists. A warm, accepting, and surprising intervention may disarm someone who would otherwise make matters more difficult.

Example: To the reluctant, dictatorial father of a court-ordered family with a sullen, delinquent son and a motivated mother: "I'd feel mad, too, about having to be here against your will. I'm surprised that you're willing to come under these circumstances and at how hard you've already worked at this problem." (All of these were true statements for the therapist.) Attention was then shifted primarily to the mother as the most motivated client.

3. *Having joined each patient, identify the genuine clients in the room and direct most of your energy to them.*

4. *Beware of working harder than patients to achieve results.* There are times and problems when you need to work especially hard to engage someone, say, with severe psychomotor slowing from depression. If there is no eventual movement, however, particularly if medication or other interventions have been competently tried, this may be a sign that you have mistaken someone as a client for change who is, in fact, not.

The essential responsibility for change is the client's. Work more from the stance of a consultant than an expert. Variously pose the question, "How can I help?" rather than communicating that you necessarily have the answers to people's problems. Of course, if you think you do have the answers to clients' problems, and they ask for them, courtesy and efficiency dictate straightforward responses. These should be framed, however, as your own ideas, which patients are absolutely under no obligation to adopt.

5. *Go in the direction of "resistance."* Use this when people seem deeply attached to their behavior, even if they've tried ostensibly to change it (see Ascher, 1989). There may be sufficient secondary gain operating to make further change efforts destructive. This intervention may set up a kind of cognitive dissonance as clients now have to justify for themselves—rather than to someone else, as is often the case—why they should keep doing the same thing. Here are two forms of this general strategy:

(a) *Restraint from change. Examples*: "It seems like you've worked so hard on this already without results that to keep going would be unwise or unfair." Or, "It seems like this is a particularly difficult problem so we ought to go slowly to insure success." Or, "Since criticizing gets you the results you want, why would you want to give it up?"

(b) *Symptom prescription. Example*: To a rebellious teen: "It's important that you keep asserting yourself so that your parents can learn to set limits." (This is also a restraint from change and a reframing of rebellious behavior as an emancipation issue.)

6. *Keep trying to reframe the problem.* In addition to the uses indicated previously, this can be especially helpful in trying to accept the unacceptable, a task that can keep people in treatment lengthily, unhappily, and unsuccessfully.

Example: A man with multiple sclerosis wanted to "accept" his disease, which turned out to be an impossible task, in part because of an inability to define acceptance. His lack of acceptance of MS was then explored as being helpful to him (it kept him trying courageously to have the "normal" life he desired).

7. *Find a different problem to work on.* The chance to experience therapy working in one respect may facilitate change in other areas. This is a common tactic, for example, in panic-disordered clients with agoraphobia. They may not, at the moment of truth, be willing to practice desensitization in an avoided restaurant, but would do so in order to drive a car because they need transportation.

8. *Expand the system.* Bring in other parties with some potential interest in the problem who may shed some light on it. *Example*: A young woman was treated pharmacologically for an atypical impulse control/seizure disorder with limited success. She was asked to bring her mother to therapy. The mother noted that "everyone in our family has a temper like that," thus confirming the therapist's suspicion that much of the client's behavior seemed interpersonal and tantrum-like.

9. *Make sure that you've capitalized on exceptions or contradictions to a problem. Example*: "I still don't understand how you are able to control your rage at work but you can't at home. What do you do that helps at work?" The client may then say something about the anticipated consequences of his behavior slowing him down. This process can then be elaborated and generalized to other settings.

10. *Have the client predict the future consequences of not changing as well as of doing something different. Example*: "What do you think will happen if things keep going the same way for a year? How would that be different if you were to do X instead?" Have the client list the pros and cons of changing.

11. *Use "circular" questioning when there appears to be no clear client* (see Johnson, 1989). This may be especially useful with volatile people or families who are not yet clients. Like fly-fishing on a hot day, this takes some skill and patience. Cast questions in a gentle, measured way as you look for something that might give you or the clients a perspective on a problem that someone is willing to act on. If you get a nibble somewhere, cast again in the same spot.

Examples: Who made the decision for you to come? What made you decide? Who is working hardest on the problem? Who would notice changes first? What would they say about it? How would you notice things were different? What's the smallest change you'd notice that would make a difference? What would it mean to you if your husband changed? If we could find a way for you to be happier without your husband changing, would that be just as good? What difference would it make to you if your wife stopped nagging? What have you done that you notice seems to affect her behavior? Would you be willing to try that some more?

Tip: Note that the effect of the questions above is to move from the externalization of a problem toward its internalization in an effort to find "ownership." Earlier, non-clients were described as seeing the solutions to their problems as outside of themselves. In contrast, when you have a genuine client with an internalized problem, try to externalize the problem.

12. *Consider whether you're focusing more on the problem than on solutions.* Beware of getting bogged down in so many details of a problem that you're looking down with the client instead of seeking a way out of a problem. Your own awareness of an overwhelming "process" may be a tip that you do not yet have a client, or at least a focused one. If you don't, return to the interventions that may work best with non-clients. If you do have a client, start emphasizing solution formation.

13. *Consider any missed opportunities for confrontation or interpretation of behavior that may be undermining potential treatment gains.* Interpretation simply tries to clarify meanings while confrontation is designed to foster both insight and a meaningful experience in a non-hostile way (Orlinsky & Howard, 1986).

Confrontation and interpretation can be risky due to their high potential for inaccuracy, misunderstanding, escalation of tension, or client drop-out (see Henry, Strupp, Schact, & Gaston, 1994). Handled skilfully, however, they may be successful in motivating some reluctant but persistent patients.

14. *Find a good consultant to help you improve your work with these situations.* This is especially important if you have difficulty holding a balanced or professionally appropriate emotional distance with clients.

15. *Bring a sense of humor about life and a basic enjoyment in doing psychotherapy itself to work with you.* The undying gratitude of clients and unqualified praise of colleagues are rare, if not fickle, rewards.

Strategies When It Appears There Is Ultimately No Client

1. *Explain the practical limits of psychotherapy:*

(a) Consider a direct statement to this effect: "We have found that psychotherapy does not work well with trying to change someone's behavior other than your own" (or whatever problem it may be that does not seem amenable to change). It is important, if blame must be found, to point to the nature of the problem or the limits of psychotherapy, not the client. Even direct confrontations of client behavior need not be shaming and may keep the door open for future positive collaboration.

(b) Consider a more indirect approach such as a "bad luck" conceptualization or something to this effect: "I'm not sure why you're in therapy since this problem has nothing to do with you and there's nothing you can do about it. This seems to me to be a case of plain bad luck [or perhaps "bad timing"] which therapy can't help." Patients may thus be encouraged to justify how therapy can help them (Johnson, 1991a).

2. *Consider a referral if you have not done so already. However, this should NOT be done when the likely result is that another therapist will simply inherit your problem.* This is how patients get passed unhappily around a system.

3. *Consider using a "contract" to dismiss non-compliant patients "for cause"* (see Richardson & Austad, 1991). This can probably be avoided if a therapist can kindly, but systematically, take clients through everything that has been tried without benefit and observe the folly of continuing.

6

_____

Special Topics

Rather than presenting the following topics comprehensively, this chapter is meant to give you some idea of how brief therapy principles can be integrated into various aspects of clinical practice. You are encouraged to pursue some of the references in the bibliography or additional resources to add to your understanding.

Before proceeding to other topics, a word is in order about the parameters of brief treatment.

CONTRAINDICATIONS FOR BRIEF THERAPY

Anybody who goes to a psychiatrist ought to have his head examined.

—*Sam Goldwyn*

The literature discussing contraindications for BT (as opposed to other approaches) finds no substantial connections to demographic or empirical data (see Bloom, 1992; Budman & Gurman, 1988). This is not to suggest that brief therapy is appropriate for all clients. It does, however, suggest that exclusions from brief treatment may actually describe the parameters of success for any psychotherapy, the advantages of which sometimes appear oversold (see LeShan, 1990).

Existing exclusionary criteria for BT are primarily associated with psychodynamic authors and are theoretically, rather than empirically, based. Mostly, these refer to severe, chronic psychopathology (including some personality disorders), lack of reality testing, a history (presumably lengthy or diverse) of unsuccessful psychotherapy, and inadequate motivation for change. Strategic therapies, on the other hand, do not exclude anything that can be acknowledged and defined specifically as a problem (Cade & O'Hanlon, 1993; Madanes, 1981).

To the extent that success with problems of the kind above is possible, it is likely to be circumscribed and contingent on felicitous variations in patient presentation and therapist orientation and skill.

It can also be argued that if severe psychopathology can be changed, it occurs through focused, sometimes intensive, incremental, and probably intermittent efforts over time. This is consonant with BT principles and incompatible only with those few forms emphasizing strict time limits as an essential feature. In other words, brief therapy is worth trying first if psychotherapy generally is considered a viable treatment option.

A more controversial consideration in correcting the notion that BT is contraindicated for severe problems lies in asking who benefits by excluding "difficult" patients from this kind of treatment. One possible beneficiary is the therapist who is uncomfortable with BT. Contraindications thus may become a matter of the clinician's comfort, not the patients' need or potential benefit.

WORKING WITH FAMILIES, COUPLES, AND CHILDREN

A complete detailing of BT approaches to couples and families is beyond the scope of this book. However, the BT assumptions, principles, and approaches outlined in the previous chapters are readily extended to the realm of family, couples, and child treatment (e.g., Bloom, 1992; Budman & Gurman, 1988; Budman et al., 1992; Gurman & Kniskern, 1991; Hudson & O'Hanlon, 1992; Kreilkamp, 1989; Selekman, 1991; Todd & Selekman, 1991; Wells & Gianetti, 1993, 1990; Weeks & Treat, 1992). As with individual treatment, significant therapeutic change can occur and persist in children and families in much less time than is commonly thought necessary (see, for example, Smyrnios & Kirby, 1993).

BT approaches to family treatment have much in common with dominant perspectives in pediatric behavioral medicine which operate from this viewpoint (Dixon & Stein, 1992):

1. Child behavior is treated as "normal" until proven otherwise.
2. Strengths are defined and utilized in the child, family, and environment. While genuine deficits and difficulties exist in children, not all problems can be remedied, and energy is best spent in areas where there are "capacities and energies" (Brazelton, 1975).
3. Variations in development are recognized, respected, and enjoyed for the definition that they give to our

understanding of human behavior, as in this example from family court:

Q. And, lastly, Gary, all your responses must be oral. Okay?

A. Oral.

Q. How old are you?

A. Oral.

(This is also a good illustration of why children are not given large amounts of individual time in brief family therapy.)

4. Helpers serve as consultants to parents in their own problem-solving. Parents are viewed as the vehicle of change for children since children are often visitors or complainants rather than clients. Moreover, parental confidence and competence are to be encouraged and built upon through a mutual relationship with the consultant and their own efforts to address common childhood and family problems (e.g., Schaefer & Millman, 1982).

The following principles are offered as a convergence of thinking about brief family therapy:

1. Functional families have problems, but these do not paralyze or rigidify their coping. Families are most expeditiously treated as unique systems. Functional family systems optimally reflect the following dimensions: open attitudes, respect for individuality, frank communication, clear hierarchies, flexible control, and spontaneous interaction (Skynner, 1981). These dimensions may be used as a treatment context and are possibly enhanced or built upon through brief treatment. They are not necessarily the explicit or specific goals of therapy.

2. Within this context, dysfunctional behavior is typically

viewed as interactionally determined. Look for interactional coping patterns that are inadequate for a given situation or developmental transition (Budman & Gurman, 1988; Cade & O'Hanlon, 1993).

3. Brief family treatment is focused treatment, usually on an explicit problem with collaboratively defined objectives. This has two important implications:

   (a) The proper identification of clients, complainants, and visitors is essential to tailoring interventions appropriately. There is often more than one type of client in family treatment; also, the identified patient is not necessarily the person seeking change. Only rarely, for example, does a youth come into treatment declaring "I'm defiant and I want to change" (Phelps, 1993, p. 297).

   Similarly, in couples treatment, at least one partner commonly desires to change the behavior of the other. Alternatively, a partner may be so ambivalent about commitment as to make couples treatment unfeasible. It is the therapist's task in family work to intervene constructively in behavior that is invalidating, blaming, or lacking in personal accountability as these dynamics tend to foreclose the possibility of constructive change (Hudson & O'Hanlon, 1992).

   (b) The development of focus is an expansion of principles elaborated earlier but in a relational context. Here are some examples of useful assessment questions to develop focus and determine motivation for change (Bergman, 1985; de Shazer, 1988; O'Hanlon & Weiner-Davis, 1989):

   Why is the family or couple coming in NOW? Who has the problem? What is the each person's understanding (framework) of the problem? Does everyone see it the same way? Who is most reactive to the problem? How willing is each person to work on the problem?

Treatment of fairly circumscribed symptoms or complaints may become focused with symptom questions:

How often does the symptom (complaint) happen? When? Where? How long does it last? Who does what in response? How effective is this? When does the symptom not happen?

Goal development may be facilitated by variations of questions posed for individual treatment:

What will be different when the family or couple is successfully done with treatment? What is the smallest increment of this that they would settle for?

Define goals specifically in behavioral terms if possible for each client. Some strategies for achieving them must be modified according to a client's status as customer, complainant, or visitor.

4. Because change is seen as occurring interpersonally and systemically in most child and family brief treatment, intrapsychic and environmental factors are given less weight. Treating children individually for any length of time assumes that they are customers in the sense described earlier, which is rarely the case. Additionally, to the extent that children are treated in isolation, the authority and competence, if not good will, of the parent(s) may be undermined. If children are engaged therapeutically, this can often be done by getting them to become customers for behavior that may get complainants "off their backs."

5. The therapist may function variously as problem solver, role model, teacher, observer, and cultivator of individuation. Transference, directives, hypnosis, role-

playing and any other tools at the therapist's disposal may be used. A primary therapist function is to make the implicit "rules" of family function more explicit and thus more amenable to change.

BRIEF THERAPY GROUPS

Love your neighbor, but don't pull down the hedge.

— Swiss proverb

Brief therapy groups may, in many respects, be viewed as a variant of family therapy (see Wells & Gianetti, 1990, for a review of brief group approaches). In general, BT groups are distinguished from other groups by the basic values and common treatment principles outlined in Chapter 2.

While groups are a popular treatment modality, group therapy does not yet have a *critical* therapeutic component or result that distinguishes it preferentially from individual treatment (Bergin & Garfield, 1994). Even so, potential advantages to brief group therapy include: (1) treating a number of people simultaneously, including couples, who share a similar problem which can serve as an organizing focus; and (2) using other group members as assistant therapists (Bloom, 1992). Moreover, some patients may find particular comfort in the universality of a group.

In these respects, groups may be a treatment of choice for some problems such as depression or social skills deficits in adolescents (e.g., Fine et al., 1989) or for circumscribed problems such as panic disorder that are amenable to inherently time-limited and structured treatment.

Four elements probably apply to any brief group treatment (Budman & Gurman, 1988):

1. pregroup preparation and screening;
2. establishing and maintaining focus;
3. developing group cohesion; and
4. existential factors and time limits.

Of these elements, maintaining a clear focus in a group, as with individual therapy, is arguably the hallmark of a BT group. This is probably most easily achieved in homogeneous, task-oriented groups. However, focus may be even more important for "process-oriented" groups or those routinely admitting new members, so that the group or an individual's stay does not become interminable.

For developmental reasons, group treatment of children and adolescents, particularly, should focus on current problems, corrective emotional experiences, and active participation in a change process (Scheidlinger, 1984).

Determining client suitability for a brief therapy group is, as with any group, a challenging process. However, there appear to be no clear exclusions (such as seriously disturbed or chronically mentally ill clients) for brief group treatment that would not apply to "longer-term" models provided that goals, structure, and therapist interventions are appropriately tailored to the group (Klein, 1985).

Care must be taken not to offset the potential treatment advantages of a brief therapy group by selecting inappropriate clients or using an inefficient screening process. Either of these problems will mitigate the increased efficiency or effectiveness of a brief treatment orientation.

The quality of your client selection may also have a bearing on the group's ability to work together. Because group cohesion is presumed to be one of the therapeutic characteristics and advantages of group work, it must be attended to regardless of the group's focus or degree of task-orientation. The particular challenge in brief group therapy is to maintain a focus *while* building cohesion. To this extent, brief group therapy is particularly dependent on disciplined, active intervention by therapists with good assessment skills, broad therapeutic repertoires, and the ability to establish rapport quickly (Garvin, 1990).

Existential and time factors have to do with anticipating and managing patients' variable responses to a predetermined ending for the group. For most groups, arguably more so for those with an interpersonal focus, the issue of ending requires explicit discussion and should address life after the group. This may be facilitated by establishing clear individual goals and reasonable treatment expectations at the outset.

Brief group therapy is commonly offered for 90 minutes at weekly intervals over a course of eight weeks (for skill-building groups) to more than a year for groups aimed at personality change (Budman & Gurman, 1988). However, this is by no means the only possible format for a time-sensitive group. It is presumed that for any brief therapy group that time limits are essential to, and facilitative of, the therapeutic process.

Because many clinicians have been trained in models using two facilitators, a word is in order about using this approach for brief treatment. *Using more than one professional to lead groups does not offer clear advantages from a brief treatment standpoint.* Co-led groups fit some family systems theoretical models and have the potential to make group work easier and more enjoyable for compatible therapists. Few things are more awkward or time-consuming, however, than co-leaders trying ineffectively to work out their problems with each other in the context of the group.

Co-leaders may be useful for keeping larger or more difficult groups focused, for modeling behavior, and certainly, for training purposes. However, these potential benefits should be weighed against the costs in time, money, and therapeutic results of using two clinicians.

USING FORMAL ASSESSMENT
IN BRIEF TREATMENT

Since the attitude of BT may be seen as "ready, fire, aim," the integration of formal assessment (conceivably described as "ready, ready, ready") sometimes poses an interesting dilemma. The limits and uses of testing develop particular clarity in time-sensitive settings. Here's an example:

A therapist treating a hostile, seemingly paranoid patient for the first time considered testing to determine the extent of paranoia. He then noticed that an interpreted MMPI from the previous year was already in the chart. It captured the patient's presentation beautifully, despite a lack of elevations that would have more obviously justified the interpretation. The colleague who had done the interpretation was asked how he got such a refined description from the test results. "Oh, that's easy," he replied, "I knew the guy."

Referrals for testing in psychotherapy are typically made for: (1) diagnostic clarification and (less appropriately) "confirmation"; (2) assistance in treatment planning; and (3) the detection of neurological, developmental, or cognitive difficulties.

Routine formal testing in brief therapy is inefficient and unnecessary because:

1. Many patients can be done with treatment in the same amount of time it would take to complete, score, interpret, and review their testing with them.
2. Diagnosis and treatment involve a continuous process

of assessment. The practice of testing for concurrent validity, that is, "making sure" that we accurately diagnose or understand a patient before trying treatment, suggests that we cannot trust ourselves or the patient to make therapeutic adjustments following immediate, thoughtful interventions based on initial data.

Moreover, apart from questions regarding the value of test-based diagnosis, there is disagreement about the constructs that many psychological tests measure. The lack of an objective "gold standard" for many disorders, especially those of personality, makes test-based diagnosis controversial.

3. Efficient testing in BT ought to add incremental validity to treatment; that is, it should not only confirm (or disconfirm) a treatment perspective, but also advance the therapy.

4. The diagnostic details important to any psychotherapy are typically available to skillful questioning and observation (Zubin, 1989). In BT, important details typically include client conceptualizations of a problem, prior efforts to change, patterns of coping, and motivation to do something different.

5. Patients' perceptions of a problem may bear little resemblance to the way problems are defined by test data. Much testing is normative and descriptive, while treatment is tailored to clients based on uniquely formulated theories about their problems. Problems identified by testing may be of varying concern to the patient.

In light of these considerations, the following suggestions may help you use testing productively in brief treatment:

1. If you are "stuck" with a patient, a short consultation with a skilled colleague or supervisor before testing

may facilitate more useful interventions. Testing is not going to show you how to do a specific intervention anyway.

2. Consider whether the patient is really a customer rather than a visitor or complainant. Testing has never done anybody's changing for them.

3. Suspected neurological problems or cognitive deficits should be promptly referred for testing. These difficulties can inhibit psychotherapy effectiveness and may require other kinds of intervention.

4. Use formal assessment in therapy strategically rather than for concurrent validity. That is, use test results to move a client toward a desirable response with respect to the client's understanding of the problem. *Always review test results with patients and use nonpathological language when doing so.*

5. If you like routine testing, consider using briefer tests with specific clinical utility and reasonable statistical power versus longer, broad-spectrum tests or batteries. For longer tests, consider using computer scoring or protocols, if such programs are available and well-done.

6. Become familiar with the uses, limits, and language of testing.

Multiculturalism and Brief Therapy

Anybody who wishes to diminish the brotherly affection of two sister countries is an enemy to both nations.

— *Sir Boyle Roach*

A thorough discussion of working briefly with different cultures is beyond the scope of this book. However, the rapidly changing demographics in the United States necessitate attention to this subject, which technically refers to African-Americans, Asian-Americans, Latino-Americans, and American Indians. (There would probably also be votes among some parents to include teenagers.) Sexual orientation and gender differences will not be discussed in this context.

In the same way that any therapy may be facilitated by an implicit understanding of a client's problem, therapy with patients of different cultures might benefit from the therapist's acquiring culturally specific knowledge or skills. Unfortunately, this can be a lengthy process, for which the needs of many patients cannot wait. Furthermore, contemporary notions of multiculturalism have tended to oversimplify relations between racial and ethnic groups, which, from the perspective of history, reveal few simple patterns (see Sowell, 1994).

This complexity extends to the study and practice of psychotherapy with ethnic minorities, where the question of what treatment works best with what clients under what conditions remains largely unanswered.

Despite the lack of rigorous research and unique methodological challenges (such as separating cultural effects from other factors in treatment), there are suggestions that certain conditions may be related to working effectively with different cultures. These are quite compatible with the "constructivist' sensibilities of BT and include:

1. Ethnic similarity between clients and therapists of *some* minority groups or individuals.
2. Using culturally responsive forms of treatment.
3. Pretherapy intervention and education with prospective clients.
4. Therapist training in cultural awareness and the culturally specific manifestations of problems.

5. Therapist sensitivity to the *heterogeneity* of ethnic minority groups (Sue, Zane, & Young, 1994).

A review of the general BT principles noted in Chapter 2 suggests that they are also compatible with the concepts of credibility and giving (Sue & Zane, 1987), which may underlie any effective treatment of different cultures and ethnic groups.

Credibility needs to be achieved rapidly to help insure treatment continuity. It is accomplished through: (1) congruence of problem conceptualization; (2) culturally compatible means of problem resolution (suggesting the need to learn how a problem might typically be handled in a particular culture); and (3) mutually agreed upon goals for treatment.

Giving involves providing some immediate treatment benefit or "gifts," even in the first session. These gifts may include "anxiety reduction, depression relief, cognitive clarity, normalization, reassurance, hope and faith, skills acquisition, a coping perspective, and goal setting" (Sue & Zane, 1987, p. 42).

Here are some additional tips if you are going to be working multiculturally:

1. Learn something about the history, rituals, and philosophies of the culture, especially with regard to issues you may see in treatment. These might include the role of "healers," the family, and dominant belief or value systems. There may be ways to incorporate these explicitly into a brief treatment approach. For example, relatively unacculturated Asian clients may not distinguish between physical and emotional symptoms in the way that other clients do. There is no reason, however, that helpful interventions cannot be constructed within this framework.

2. It may be advisable, as with any client, to inquire about

the client's familiarity with therapy and comfort seeking help from someone who may not know much about the client's culture. An expressed willingness to understand someone better may enhance mutual understanding and lead to productive work or a more appropriate referral.

3. Refrain from rigid assumptions that you cannot help someone because you are culturally different or, conversely, that you necessarily understand someone's problems because you share a similar cultural or ethnic background. Remember that there are limits to cultural or ethnic assumptions as applied to individuals.

MEDICATION AND BRIEF THERAPY

> Trying to treat depression [pharmacologically] without treating the [relationship] distress is like trying to treat hayfever when the patient works in a flower shop.
>
> —*E. Yeats (1989, p. 54)*

A significant trend in mental health is to treat psychological problems as "biopsychosocial"; that is, as having multiple, interactive components (see, for example, Barlow, 1988). A further corollary of this thinking is the simultaneous, if not primary, reliance on medication in treatment.

However, some forms of brief psychotherapy are as effective as medication, if not more so, in the treatment of most problems, either by themselves or in combined approaches (see, for example, Hollon & Beck, 1994). Issues of relative efficiency, cost, patient comfort, and therapist skill in treating particular problems then become important factors to consider.

With respect to depression, for example, standard cognitive-behavioral treatment may take longer in some cases to reach a "therapeutic dose" than medication, but potentially offers greater relapse prevention and more rapid intervention with hopelessness (e.g., Hollon et al., 1992). In contrast, solution-focused brief therapy shows the promise of achieving results more quickly than either (4.6 visits average across diagnostic categories), but it remains to be tested in controlled situations (de Shazer, 1991b; Johnson & Miller, 1994).

It is important to keep in mind that what is effective in controlled studies is not necessarily efficacious in practice. Also worth noting is that the controlled research itself used to document antidepressant medication effects, for example, has come under compelling criticism (Greenberg, Bornstein, Greenberg, & Fisher, 1992a; 1992b).

Genuine treatment effects notwithstanding, potential medication problems (many shared with psychotherapy) include variability in practitioner skill and accessibility, cost, enormous levels of patient noncompliance, rebound effects (for some benzodiazepines), physical or psychological dependence, undesirable side effects including overdose, metabolic variation in patients, length of time required for therapeutic effect, and relapse prevention. For some patients, taking medication also undermines their sense of personal responsibility or control.

Some Guidelines for Making Medication Referrals

There are no easy ways to acquire the clinical judgment necessary in making sound referrals for medication. Clinician preferences are probably shaped as much by training, experience, and beliefs as by clinical literature. Medicating every complaint with an acknowledged biochemical basis makes no more sense (since all behavior has a biological basis) than never medicating.

Here are some tips for making useful medication referrals in brief treatment:

1. Learn about psychopharmacology and the biological bases of behavior. Your practice will be better for it.
2. Consider medication more strongly if:
   (a) the patient requests it for an appropriate problem;
   (b) the patient has had a prior positive response to medication;
   (c) the patient has a history of poor response to well-done psychotherapy;
   (d) the patient's family history is "loaded" for a problem responsive to medications;
   (e) the clinical literature supports medication as a first choice for the problem (e.g., bipolar or schizophrenic spectrum disorders);
   (f) the severity or chronicity of symptoms is particularly pronounced.
3. *Do not* make a medication referral for problems simply because you don't know what to do with them and one option is to medicate. Get a good psychotherapy consult for yourself first or, better yet, develop your skills in working with similar problems.
4. For problems where either or both medication and therapy are possibilities, try a session or two of therapy first to see if improvement is noted. The thinking here is to capitalize on BT's "catalytic" components, which may serve to accelerate change (Eckert, 1993).

BECOMING A BRIEF THERAPIST

Because BT tries to accomplish more with less, it is often presumed to require less of clinicians. In reality, the opposite is true. Effective brief therapists must make many thoughtful and difficult decisions rapidly, without

rushing the therapy. This is something that usually benefits from experience, continuing education, and practice.
For those therapists who persist, the rewards can be significant, including an ability to manage large, difficult, or
varied caseloads comfortably, and making a difference to
most people quickly and tangibly. Here are some tips to
guide the way:

1. *Carefully consider the attitudes and beliefs that guide
   your work with clients.* Cross-reference them with the
   BT values listed in Chapter 2. If they are relatively
   incompatible, consider how willing you are to challenge
   the present basis of your work.
2. *Study, systematically if possible, various perspectives
   of human behavior, including approaches and techniques not commonly associated with BT.* Object relations training, for example, might usefully heighten
   your awareness and understanding of interpersonal
   processes. Read literature about people that transcends
   time and culture. The works of Dostoevsky, Dickens,
   or Maya Angelou are, for most people, more interesting reading than professional textbooks or journals
   (which you are also encouraged to consult), and frequently more revealing in their observations about human nature.
3. *Consider being a client yourself for some problem that
   might benefit from therapy.* Pay attention to what is
   more or less helpful in this process as it may inform
   your own work with clients.
4. *Question authority.* Do not accept everything about a
   therapeutic approach, even an established one, as the
   only way to proceed in treatment. Learn to think criti-
   cally about the most useful and rigorous aspects of
   an approach while striving toward a clearly defined,
   continuously evolving personal model of therapy.
5. *Take risks.* Try new things in therapy (with consulta-

tion, if necessary) even if you're not an expert. (How else do you get to be an expert?) For example, a new quasi-hypnotic technique with an as yet unknown curative mechanism, eye movement desensitization and reprocessing (EMDR; Lipke & Botkin, 1992; Shapiro, 1989), is easily learned and can produce strikingly rapid reduction in PTSD symptoms. Such things are worth a try.

6. *Develop broad competencies.* Apart from trying new techniques, a willingness to work with various kinds of people or problems is also desirable from a BT standpoint. This can keep your work fresh and challenging, make you more useful to more people, and limit unnecessary referrals to other clinicians. It cannot be emphasized enough.

   If you consistently avoid some aspects of clinical practice, consider seeking assistance until you can function more confidently and comfortably with them. Your therapeutic work generally is likely to improve as a consequence.

7. *Pace the integration of BT ideas and techniques.* Try something, analyze its effect, make adjustments as necessary, and try it again until it is incorporated or discarded from your work. Develop a personal feedback loop.

8. *Get the best supervision and consultation you can afford.* It is also advisable, especially in peer or group supervision, to structure the consultation in ways that facilitate brief interventions with clients. Bring a disciplined focus to the supervision by routinely asking colleagues questions such as these: What can we help you with? Why is this case being staffed now? What does the patient want from therapy? What interventions have been tried with what results? This will help reinforce a similar process with clients.

Glossary

Brief therapy: Therapy with various forms but characterized by the planned use of specific concepts and principles in a focused, purposeful way. It emphasizes efficiency as well as efficacy. Underlying its variety, BT shares a set of clinical features and a value orientation.

Brief dynamic therapy: Therapies generally distinguished by the selection of motivated, functional patients; the use of transference and countertransference; the confrontation and interpretation of focal, intrapsychic conflict; and emphasis on the psychological importance of termination.

Circular questioning: A process of measured questioning designed to elicit more information and unthreateningly guide patients to new recognitions, empathic understanding, or different behavior. Especially useful when either therapist or clients are stuck.

Collaboration: Refers to the process of establishing treatment goals and outcomes that are satisfactory to patients. The therapist is in charge of the collaboration.

Complainants: Patients who acknowledge a problem exists but do not see themselves as part of a solution. Often described as "difficult" clients because they are genuinely distressed but commonly blaming or helpless. The solutions to their problems are seen as existing outside of themselves.

Cognitive-behavioral therapy: Relies on a variety of empirically-based techniques to achieve mutually determined goals. Strives for self-efficacy and relief of current problems through challenging faulty cognitions and their behavioral correlates. Often employs social-learning paradigms.

Customers: True clients. Characterized by the acknowledgment of a problem and a willingness to work on it. Customers for change see themselves as being part of a solution.

Homework: Assignments designed to facilitate progress between sessions. Broadly considered, it develops skills or disturbs the system in which clients function and in which they are presumably "stuck."

Interpersonal therapy: Explicitly treats problems, especially depression, as being maintained by problematic relationships.

Long-term therapy: Recapitulating one's history with a (presumably) stable figure.

Paradoxical intention: A variety of interventions, including humor, designed to be surprising and contrary to client expectations. Often used with entrenched behavior in which client efforts to solve the problem make it worse. Prescription of a symptom is an example.

Reframing: A universal therapeutic technique, critical to BT. Generally, a therapist-induced change in perspective which often leads clients to corresponding changes in attitude and behavior. Look especially for positive intentions behind problematic behavior, the positive function of symptoms, or their positive unintended consequences.

Restraints from change: Techniques used when there is a danger of a therapist working harder than clients or clients are ambivalent about changing.

Solution-focused brief therapy: A particularly economical derivative of systemic therapy. It emphasizes the therapeutic use of questions, building on exceptions to problems, and rapid transitions to solutions intrinsic to a problem or client.

Strategic therapy: Generally refers to specific therapist-initiated interventions designed for specific problems. Sees problems as often maintained by efforts to change them. Symptoms are often treated as having a function. Change is effected primarily through treating a specific symptom. Implicitly systemic and interpersonal.

Structural therapy: Seeks to create a change in immediate problems through altering transactional processes in a family system.

Systemic therapy: Therapy that treats problems via a relationship or interaction. Systems theory relies on the ideas that the whole is larger than the sum of parts, that the system tends to resist change (homeostasis), and that changing one part of a system will affect other parts. All therapy should properly be considered systemic.

Visitors: Patients who do not acknowledge that there is a problem. Often brought in to therapy by complainants.

Bibliography

Adams, J. F., Piercy, F. P., & Jurich, A. (1991). Effects of solution focused therapy's "formula first session task" on compliance and outcome in family therapy. *Journal of Marital and Family Therapy, 17,* 277–290.

Alexander, F., & French, T. M. (1946). *Psychoanalytic therapy: Principles and applications.* New York: Ronald Press.

Aponte, H. J. (1992). The black sheep of the family: A structural approach to brief therapy. In S. H. Budman, M. F. Hoyt, & S. Friedman (Eds.), *The first session in brief therapy* (pp. 324–345). New York: Guilford.

Aronson, E. (1992). *The social animal* (6th ed.). New York: Freeman.

Ascher, L. M. (Ed.) (1989). *Therapeutic paradox.* New York: Guilford.

Auden, W. H., & Kronenberger, L. (Eds.) (1962). *The Viking book of aphorisms.* New York: Dorset Press.

Barlow, D. H. (1988). *Anxiety and its disorders: The nature and treatment of anxiety and panic.* New York: Guilford.

Barlow, D. H., & Craske, M. G. (1989). *Mastery of your anxiety and panic.* Albany, NY: Graywind Publications.

93

Beck, A. T. (1976). *Cognitive therapy and emotional disorders*. New York: International Universities Press.

Beck, A. T., Freeman, A. et al. (1990). *Cognitive therapy of personality disorders*. New York: Guilford.

Beck, A. T., Wright, F. D., & Newman, C. F. (1992). Cocaine abuse. In A. Freeman & F. M. Dattilio (Eds.), *Comprehensive casebook of cognitive therapy* (pp. 185–192). New York: Plenum.

Beier, E. G., & Young, D. M. (1984). *The silent language of psychotherapy* (2nd ed.). New York: Aldine de Gruyter.

Bennett, M. J. (1988). The greening of the HMO: Implications for prepaid psychiatry. *American Journal of Psychiatry, 145*, 1544–1549.

Berg, I. K., & Miller, S. D. (1992a). *Dying well: A case presentation of solution-focused therapy*. Audiotape. Milwaukee: Brief Family Therapy Center.

Berg, I. K., & Miller, S. D. (1992b). *Working with the problem drinker: A solution-focused approach*. New York: Norton.

Bergin, A. E., & Garfield, S. L. (1994). Overviews, trends and future issues. In A. E. Bergin & S. L. Garfield (Eds.), *Handbook of psychotherapy and behavior change* (4th ed.) (pp. 821–830). New York: Wiley.

Bergman, J. S. (1985). *Fishing for barracuda: Pragmatics of brief systemic therapy*. New York: Norton.

Berkman, A. S., Bassos, C. A., & Post, L. (1988). Managed mental care and independent practice: A challenge to psychology. *Psychotherapy: Theory, Research, and Practice, 25*, 449–454.

Beutler, L. E. (1991). Have all won and must all have prizes? Revisiting Luborsky et al.'s verdict. *Journal of Consulting and Clinical Psychology, 59*, 1–7.

Beutler, L. E., Crago, M., & Arizmendi, T. G. (1986). Therapist variables in psychotherapy process and outcome. In S. L. Garfield & A. E. Bergin (Eds.), *Handbook of psychotherapy and behavior change* (3rd ed.) (pp. 257–310). New York: Wiley.

Black, E. (1981, November 12). Practice of RET is as rational as saying your ABCs. *Minneapolis Tribune*, pp. 1C, 4C.

Bloom, B. L. (1990). Managing mental health services: Some comments on the overdue debate in psychology. *Community Mental Health Journal, 26*(1), 107–124.

Bloom, B. L. (1992). *Planned short-term psychotherapy: A clinical handbook*. Boston: Allyn & Bacon.

Brazelton, T. B. (1975). Anticipatory guidance. *Pediatric Clinics of North America, 222*, 533–544.

Broderick, C. B. & Schrader, S. S. (1981). The history of professional marriage and family therapy. In A. S. Gurman & D. P. Kniskern (Eds.), *Handbook of family therapy* (pp. 5–38). New York: Brunner/Mazel.

Broskowski, A. (1991). Current mental health care environments: Why managed care is necessary. *Professional Psychology: Research and Practice, 22*(1), 6–14.

Budman, S. (1989, August). *Training experienced clinicians to do brief treatment — silk purses into sow's ears.* Paper presented at the 97th annual convention of the American Psychological Association, New Orleans, LA.

Budman, S. H., & Gurman, A. S. (1988). *Theory and practice of brief therapy.* New York: Guilford.

Budman, S. H., Hoyt, M. F., & Friedman, S. (Eds.) (1992). *The first session in brief therapy.* New York: Guilford.

Burns, D. D. (1990). *The feeling good handbook.* New York: Plume.

Butler, S. F., Strupp, H. H., & Binder, J. L. (1992). Time-limited dynamic psychotherapy. In S. H. Budman, M. F. Hoyt, & S. Friedman, *The first session in brief therapy* (pp. 87–110). New York: Guilford.

Cade, B., & O'Hanlon, W. H. (1993). *A brief guide to brief therapy.* New York: Norton.

Cooper, J. F., & Thelen, M. (1991). *Preferred provider organizations and independent practice organizations in managed health care: Implications for mental health practitioners.* Unpublished manuscript.

Crits-Cristoph, P., & Barber, J. P (Eds.) (1991). *Handbook of short-term dynamic psychotherapy.* New York: Basic Books.

Csikszentmihalyi, M. (1990). *Flow: The psychology of optimal experience.* New York: HarperPerennial.

Davanloo, H. (1979). Techniques of short-term psychotherapy. *Psychiatric Clinics of North America, 2*, 11–22.

de Shazer, S. (1985). *Keys to solution in brief therapy.* New York: Norton.

de Shazer, S. (1988). *Clues: Investigating solutions in brief therapy.* New York: Norton.

de Shazer, S. (1991a). Foreword. In Y. M. Dolan, *Resolving sexual abuse.* New York: Norton.

de Shazer, S. (1991b). *Putting difference to work.* New York: Norton.

Derogatis, L. (1983). *SCL-90-R Manual II.* Towson, MD: Clinical Psychometric Research.

Dixon, S. D., & Stein, M. S. (1992). *Encounters with children: Pediatric behavior and development* (2nd ed.). St. Louis: Mosby-Year Book.

Dolan, Y. M. (1991). *Resolving sexual abuse.* New York: Norton.

Donovan, J. M. (1987). Brief dynamic psychotherapy: Toward a more comprehensive model. *Psychiatry, 50,* 167–183.

Dossey, L. (1993). *Healing words.* New York: HarperCollins.

Dubovsky, S. L. (1993, September). *Treatment resistant depression: Psychotherapy and pharmacology.* Paper presented at annual meeting of Park Nicollet Medical Center, Minneapolis, MN.

Eckert, P. (1993). Acceleration of change: Catalysts in brief therapy. *Clinical Psychology Review, 13*(3), 241–253.

Ellis, A. (1992). Brief therapy: The rational-emotive method. In S. H. Budman, M. F. Hoyt, & S. Friedman (Eds.), *The first session in brief therapy* (pp. 36–59). New York: Guilford.

Ellis, A., & Grieger, R. (Eds.) (1977). *Handbook of rational-emotive therapy* (Vol. 1). New York: Springer.

Epperson, D. L., Bushway, D. J., & Warman, R. E. (1983). Client self-terminations after one counseling session: Effects of problem recognition, counselor gender, and counselor experience. *Journal of Counseling Psychology, 30*, 307–315.

Ferenczi, S. (1920). The further development of an active therapy in psychoanalysis. In J. Richman (Ed.) (1960), *Further contributions to the theory and techniques of psychoanalysis* (pp. 198–216). London: Hogarth.

Fine, S., Gilbert, M., Schmidt, L., Haley, G., Maxwell, A., & Forth, A. (1989). Short-term group therapy with depressed adolescent outpatients. *Canadian Journal of Psychiatry, 34*, 97–102.

Fisch, R. (1990). The broader interpretation of Milton Erickson's work. In S. Lankton (Ed.), *The Ericksonian monographs, No. 7, The issue of broader implications of Ericksonian therapy* (pp. 1–5). New York: Brunner/Mazel.

Fisch, R., Weakland, J., & Segal, L. (1982). *The tactics of change: Doing therapy briefly*. San Francisco: Jossey-Bass.

Frank, J. D. (1974). *Persuasion and healing*. New York: Schocken.

Freeman, A., & Dattilio, F. M. (Eds.) (1992). *Comprehensive casebook of cognitive therapy*. New York: Plenum.

Friedman, S. (1992). Constructing solutions (stories) in brief family therapy. In S. H. Budman, M. F. Hoyt, & S. Friedman (Eds.), *The first session in brief therapy* (pp. 282–306). New York: Guilford.

Garfield, S. L. (1978). Research on client variables in psychotherapy. In S. L. Garfield & A. E. Bergin (Eds.), *Handbook of psychotherapy and behavior change* (2nd ed.) (pp. 271–298). New York: Wiley.

Garfield, S. L. (1986). Research on client variables in psychotherapy. In S. L. Garfield & A. E. Bergin (Eds.), *Handbook of psychotherapy and behavior change* (3rd ed.) (pp. 213–256). New York: Wiley.

Garfield, S. L. (1994). Research on client variables in psychotherapy. In A. E. Bergin & S. L. Garfield (Eds.), *Handbook of psychotherapy and behavior change* (4th ed.) (pp. 190–229). New York: Wiley.

Garvin, C. D. (1990). Short-term group therapy. In R. A. Wells & V. J. Gianetti, (Eds.), *Handbook of the brief psychotherapies* (pp. 513–536). New York: Plenum.

Giles, T. R. (1992). Brief therapy. *Strategies and Solutions, 1*, 10–12.

Gitlin, M. J. (1990). *The psychotherapist's guide to psychopharmacology*. New York: Free Press.

Goleman, D. (1993, October 17). Placebo more powerful than was thought, study finds. *Minneapolis Star Tribune*, p. 17E.

Greenberg, R. P., Bornstein, R. F., Greenberg, M. D., & Fisher, S. (1992a). A meta-analysis of antidepressant outcome under "blinder" conditions. *Journal of Consulting and Clinical Psychology, 60*, 664–669.

Greenberg, R. P., Bornstein, R. F., Greenberg, M. D., & Fisher, S. (1992b). As for the kings: A reply with regard to depression subtypes and antidepressant response. *Journal of Consulting and Clinical Psychology, 60*, 675–677.

Gurman, A. S., & Kniskern, D. P. (Eds.) (1991). *Handbook of family therapy*, Vol. 2. New York: Brunner/Mazel.

Gustafson, J. P. (1986). *The complex secret of brief psychotherapy*. New York: Norton.

Haley, J. (1991). *Problem-solving therapy* (2nd ed.). San Francisco: Jossey-Bass.

Hawton, K., Salkovskis, P. M., Kirk, J., & Clark, D. M. (Eds.) (1989). *Cognitive behaviour therapy for psychiatric problems: A practical guide*. Oxford: Oxford University Press.

Henry, W. P., Strupp, H. H., Schact, T. E., & Gaston, L. (1994). Psychodynamic approaches. In A. E. Bergin & S. L. Garfield (Eds.), *Handbook of psychotherapy and behavior change* (4th ed.) (pp. 428–467). New York: Wiley.

Hollon, S. D., & Beck, A. T. (1994). Cognitive and cognitive-behavioral therapies. In A. E. Bergin & S. L. Garfield (Eds.), *Handbook of psychotherapy and behavior change* (4th ed.) (pp. 428–467). New York: Wiley.

Hollon, S. D., DeRubeis, R. J., Evans, M. D., Wiemer, M. J., Garvey, M. J., Grove, W. M., & Tuason, W. B. (1992). Cognitive therapy and pharmacotherapy for depression: Singly and in combination. *Archives of General Psychiatry, 49*, 774–781.

Howard, K. I., Kopta, S. M., Krause, M. S., & Orlinsky, D. E. (1986). The dose-effect relationship in psychotherapy. *American Psychologist, 41*, 159–164.

Hoyt, M. F. (1987). Resistance to brief therapy. *American Psychologist, 42*, 408–409.

Hoyt, M. F., Rosenbaum, R., & Talmon, M. (1992). Planned single-session psychotherapy. In S. H. Budman, M. F. Hoyt, & S. Friedman, *The first session in brief therapy* (pp. 59–86). New York: Guilford.

Hudson, P. O., & O'Hanlon, W. H. (1992). *Rewriting love stories: Brief marital therapy*. New York: Norton.

Johnson, L. D. (1989). Developments in interview techniques. Unpublished monograph.

Johnson, L. D. (1990). *Using language for change*. Unpublished monograph.

Johnson, L. D. (1991a, September). *Practical brief psychotherapy: Problems and solutions*. Workshop, St. Paul, MN.

Johnson, L. D. (1991b). *On time in brief therapy*. Unpublished monograph.

Johnson, L. D. (1992). *Homework assignments*. Unpublished monograph.

Johnson, L. D., & Miller, S. D. (1994). Modification of depression risk factors: A solution-focused approach. *Psychotherapy, 31*, 244–253.

Jones, E. E., & Pulos, S. M. (1993). Comparing the process in psychodynamic and cognitive-behavioral therapies. *Journal of Consulting and Clinical Psychology, 61*(2), 306–316.

Klein, R. H. (1985). Some principles of short-term group therapy. *International Journal of Group Psychotherapy, 35*, 309–329.

Klerman, G. L., Weissman, M. M., Rounsaville, B. J., & Chevron, E. S. (1984). *Interpersonal therapy of depression*. New York: Basic Books.

Koss, M. P., & Butcher, J. N. (1986). Research on brief therapy. In S. L. Garfield & A. E. Bergin (Eds.), *Handbook of psychotherapy and behavior change* (3rd ed.) (pp. 627–670). New York: Wiley.

Koss, M. P., & Shiang, J. (1994). Research on brief therapy. In A. E. Bergin & S. L. Garfield (Eds.), *Handbook of psychotherapy and behavior change* (4th ed.) (pp. 664–700). New York: Wiley.

Kramer, M. (1989). *Making sense of wine*. New York: Morrow.

Kreilkamp, T. (1989). *Intermittent time-limited therapy with children and families*. New York: Brunner/Mazel.

Lambert, M. J., & Bergin, A. E. (1994). The effectiveness of psychotherapy. In A. E. Bergin & S. L. Garfield (Eds.), *Handbook of psychotherapy and behavior change* (4th ed.) (pp. 143–190). New York: Wiley.

Lambert, M. J., Shapiro, D. A., & Bergin, A. E. (1986). The effectiveness of psychotherapy. In S. L. Garfield & A. E. Bergin (Eds.), *Handbook of psychotherapy and behavior change* (3rd ed.) (pp. 157–211). New York: Wiley.

Lankton, S. R., Lankton, C. H., & Matthews, W. J. (1991). Ericksonian family therapy. In A. S. Gurman & D. P. Kniskern (Eds.), *Handbook of family therapy*, Vol. 2 (pp. 239–283). New York: Brunner/Mazel.

Lazarus, L. W. (1982). Brief psychotherapy for narcissistic disturbances. *Psychotherapy, 19*, 228–236.

Lehman, A. K., & Salovey, P. (1990). An introduction to cognitive-behavior therapy. In R. A. Wells & V. J. Gianetti (Eds.) (1990), *Handbook of the brief psychotherapies* (pp. 239-259). New York: Plenum.

Leibovich, M. (1981). Short-term psychotherapy for the borderline personality disorder. *Psychotherapy and Psychosomatics, 2,* 57-64.

LeShan, L. (1990). *The dilemma of psychology.* New York: Dutton.

Levy, R. L., & Shelton, J. L. (1990). Tasks in brief therapy. In R. A. Wells & V. J. Gianetti (Eds.), *Handbook of the brief psychotherapies* (pp. 145-163). New York: Plenum.

Lipke, H. J., & Botkin, A. L. (1992). Case studies of eye movement desensitization and reprocessing (EMDR) with chronic post-traumatic stress disorder. *Psychotherapy, 29*(4), 591-594.

Logue, M. B., Sher, K. J., & Frensch, P. A. (1992). Purported characteristics of adult children of alcoholics: A possible "Barnum Effect." *Professional Psychology: Research and Practice, 23,* 226-232.

Madanes, C. (1981). *Strategic family therapy.* San Francisco: Jossey-Bass.

Mahoney, M. J. (1993). Theoretical developments in the cognitive psychotherapies. *Journal of Consulting and Clinical Psychology, 61,* 187-193.

Malan, J. (1963). *A study of brief psychotherapy.* London: Tavistock.

Mann, J. (1973). *Time-limited psychotherapy.* Cambridge: Harvard University Press.

McAuley, E., Poag, K., Gleason, A., & Wraith, S. (1990). Attrition from exercise programs: Attributional and affective perspectives. *Journal of Social Behavior and Personality, 5*(6), 591-602.

Minuchin, S., & Fishman, H. C. (1981). *Family therapy techniques.* Cambridge: Harvard University Press.

Mohl, P. C., Martinez, D., Ticknor, C., Huang, M., & Cordell, L. (1991). Early drop-outs from psychotherapy. *Journal of Nervous and Mental Disease, 179,* 478-491.

National Institute of Mental Health (1981). *Provisional data on federally funded community mental health centers 1978-79.* Report prepared by the Survey and Reports Branch, Division of Biometry and Epidemiology. Washington, DC: US Government Printing Office.

Neill, J. R., & Kniskern, D. P. (Eds.) (1982). *From psyche to system: The evolving therapy of Carl Whitaker.* New York: Guilford.

Nguyen, T. D., Atkisson, C. C., & Stegner, B. L. (1983). Assessment of patient satisfaction: Development and refinement of a service evaluation questionnaire. *Evaluation and Program Planning, 6,* 299-313.

O'Hanlon, W. H., & Wilk, J. (1987). *Shifting contexts.* New York: Guilford.

O'Hanlon, W. H., & Weiner-Davis, M. (1989). *In search of solutions: A new direction in psychotherapy.* New York: Norton.

Omer, H. (1994). *Critical interventions in psychotherapy.* New York: Norton.

Orlinsky, D. E., & Howard, K. I. (1986). Process and outcome in psychotherapy. In S. L. Garfield & A. E. Bergin (Eds.), *Handbook of psychotherapy and behavior change* (3rd ed.) (pp. 311–381). New York: Wiley.

Peake, T. H., & Borduin, C. M., & Archer, R. P. (1988). *Brief psychotherapies: Changing frames of mind.* Beverly Hills, CA: Sage.

Pekarik, G. (1983). Improvement in clients who have given different reasons for dropping out of treatment. *Journal of Clinical Psychology, 39,* 909–913.

Pekarik, G. (1990a). *Brief therapy training manual.* Topeka, KS: Washburn University.

Pekarik, G. (1990b, January). *Rationale, training, and implementation of time-sensitive treatments.* Presentation to Executive Directors, MCC Companies, Inc. Minneapolis, MN.

Pekarik, G., & Finney-Owen, G. K. (1987). Psychotherapist's attitudes and beliefs relevant to client drop-out. *Community Mental Health Journal, 23*(2), 120–130.

Pekarik, G., & Wierzbicki, M. (1986). The relationship between expected and actual psychotherapy duration. *Psychotherapy, 23,* 532–534.

Persons, J. B. (1991). Psychotherapy outcome studies do not accurately represent current models of psychotherapy. *American Psychologist, 46*(2), 99–106.

Peters, T., & Waterman, R. (1982). *In search of excellence: Lessons from America's best run companies.* New York: Harper & Row.

Phelps, P. A. (1993). The case of oppositional cooperation. In R. A. Wells & V. J. Gianetti (Eds.), *Casebook of the brief psychotherapies* (pp. 287–303). New York: Plenum.

Prochaska, J. O. (1992). In search of how people change: Applications to addictive behaviors. *American Psychologist, 47,* 1102–1114.

Reid, W. J. (1990). An integrative model for short-term treatment. In R. A. Wells & V. J. Gianetti (Eds.), *Handbook of the brief psychotherapies* (pp. 55–77). New York: Plenum.

Richardson, L. M., & Austad, C. S. (1991). Realities of mental health practice in managed care settings. *Professional Psychology: Research and Practice, 22*(1), 52–59.

Rubin, S. S., & Niemeier, D. L. (1992). Non-verbal affective communication as a factor in psychotherapy. *Psychotherapy, 29,* 596–602.

Sabin, J. E. (1991). Clinical skills for the 1990's: Six lessons from the HMO practice. *Hospital and Community Psychiatry, 42*(6), 605–608.

Sachs, J. S. (1983). Negative factors in brief psychotherapy: An empirical assessment. *Journal of Consulting and Clinical Psychology, 51*(4), 557–564.

Schaefer, C. E., & Millman, H. L. (1982). *How to help children with common problems.* St. Louis: Plume.

Scheidlinger, S. (1984). Short-term group therapy for children: An overview. *International Journal of Group Psychotherapy, 34,* 573–585.

Segal, L. (1991). Brief therapy: The MRI approach. In A. S. Gurman & D. P. Kniskern (Eds.), *Handbook of family therapy,* Vol. 2 (pp. 171–199). New York: Brunner/Mazel.

Selekman, M. D. (1991). The solution-oriented parenting group: A treatment alternative that works. *Journal of Strategic and Systemic Therapies, 10,* 37–50.

Shapiro, D. A., & Shapiro, D. (1982). Meta-analysis of comparative outcome studies: A replication and refinement. *Psychological Bulletin, 92,* 581–604.

Shapiro, F. (1989). Eye movement desensitization: A new treatment of post-traumatic stress disorder. *Journal of Behavior Therapy and Experimental Psychiatry, 20*(3), 211–217.

Shaw, B. F., Katz, J., & Siotis, I. (1993). Cognitive therapy of unipolar depression. In R. A. Wells & V. J. Gianetti (Eds.), *Casebook of the brief psychotherapies* (pp. 77–90). New York: Plenum.

Shearin, E. N., & Linehan, M. M. (1989). Dialectics and behavior therapy: A metaparadoxical approach to the treatment of borderline personality disorder. In L. M. Ascher (Ed.), *Therapeutic paradox* (pp. 255–287). New York: Guilford.

Sifneos, P. S. (1992). *Short-term anxiety-provoking therapy: A treatment manual.* New York: Basic Books.

Skynner, R. (1981). An open-systems, group-analytic approach to family therapy. In A. S. Gurman & D. P. Kniskern (Eds.), *Handbook of family therapy,* Vol. 1 (pp. 39–85). New York: Brunner/Mazel.

Sledge, W. H., Moras, K., Hartley, D., & Levine, M. (1990). Effect of time-limited therapy on patient drop-out rates. *American Journal of Psychiatry, 147,* 1341–1347.

Smith, M. L., Glass, G. V., & Miller, T. I. (1980). *The benefits of psychotherapy.* Baltimore: Johns Hopkins University Press.

Smyrnios, K. X., & Kirby, R. J. (1993). Long-term comparison of brief versus unlimited psychodynamic treatments with children and their parents. *Journal of Consulting and Clinical Psychology, 61,* 1020–1027.

Sowell, T. (1994). *Race and culture: A world view.* New York: Basic Books.

Staples, F. R., Sloan, R. D., Whipple, K., Cristol, A. H., & Yorkston,

N. (1976). Process and outcome in psychotherapy and behavior therapy. *Journal of Consulting and Clinical Psychology, 44*, 340–350.

Strupp, H. H., & Binder, J. L. (1984). *Psychotherapy in a new key: A guide to time-limited dynamic psychotherapy.* New York: Basic Books.

Sue, S., & Zane, N. (1987). The role of culture and cultural techniques in psychotherapy. *American Psychologist, 42*(1), 37–45.

Sue, S., Zane, N., & Young, K. (1994). Research on psychotherapy with culturally diverse populations. In A. E. Bergin & S. L. Garfield (Eds.), *Handbook of psychotherapy and behavior change* (4th ed.) (pp. 783–817). New York: Wiley.

Talmon, M. (1990). *Single-session therapy: Maximizing the effect of the first (and often only) therapeutic encounter.* San Francisco: Jossey-Bass.

Todd, T. C., & Selekman, M. D. (1991). *Family therapy approaches with adolescent substance abusers.* Needham Heights, MA: Allyn & Bacon.

Townsend, J. H. (1992). The task of balancing high-quality care with cost-effectiveness. *Strategies and Solutions, 1*, 12–14.

Ursano, R. J., Sonnenberg, S. M., & Lazar, S. G. (1991). *Concise guide to psychodynamic psychotherapy.* Washington, DC: American Psychiatric Press.

Walter, J. L., & Peller, J. E. (1992). *Becoming solution focused in brief therapy.* New York: Brunner/Mazel.

Watzlawick, P., Weakland, J., & Fisch, R. (1974). *Change.* New York: Norton.

Weakland, J. H., & Fisch, R. (1992). Brief therapy—MRI style. In S. H. Budman, M. F. Hoyt, & S. Friedman (Eds.), *The first session in brief therapy* (pp. 306–324). New York: Guilford.

Weeks, G. R., & Treat, S. (1992). *Couples in treatment: Techniques and approaches for effective practice.* New York: Brunner/Mazel.

Weissman, M. M., & Markowitz, J. A. (1994). Interpersonal psychotherapy: Current status. *Archives of General Psychiatry, 51*, 599–606.

Wells, R. A. (1993). Clinical strategies in brief psychotherapy. In R. A. Wells & V. J. Gianetti (Eds.), *Casebook of the brief psychotherapies* (pp. 3–17). New York: Plenum.

Wells, R. A., & Gianetti, V. J. (Eds.) (1990). *Handbook of the brief psychotherapies.* New York: Plenum.

Wells, R. A., & Gianetti, V. J. (Eds.) (1993). *Casebook of the brief psychotherapies.* New York: Plenum.

Winston, A., Laikan, M., Pollack, J., Samstag, L. W., McCullough, L., & Muran, J. C. (1994). Short-term psychotherapy of personality disorders. *American Journal of Psychiatry, 151*(2), 190–194.

Wolberg, L. R. (1980). *Handbook of short-term psychotherapy*. New York: Thieme-Stratton.

Yalom, I. (1989). *Love's executioner & other tales of psychotherapy*. New York: Harper Perennial.

Yapko, M. (1992). Therapy with direction. In S. H. Budman, M. F. Hoyt, & S. Friedman (Eds.), *The first session in brief therapy* (pp. 156–180). New York: Guilford.

Yeats, E. (1989). Pharmacotherapy from the perspective of family ecology. In J. M. Ellison (Ed.), *The psychotherapist's guide to pharmacotherapy* (pp. 51–79). St. Louis: Mosby-Year Book.

Zeig, J. (Ed.) (1982). *Ericksonian approaches to hypnosis and psychotherapy*. New York: Brunner/Mazel.

Zimet, C. N. (1989). The mental health care revolution: Will psychology survive? *American Psychologist, 44*, 703–708.

Zubin, J. (1989). Use of research instruments in psychopathological assessment: Some historical perspectives. In S. Wetzler (Ed.), *Measuring mental illness: Psychometric assessment for clinicians* (pp. 21–43). Washington, DC: American Psychiatric Press.

Index